Edited by Francis D. Costa, S. S. S.

GOD AND CHARITY:

Images of Eastern Orthodox Theology, Spirituality, and Practice

+ Father Elías Stephanopoulos

Papers by:

Thomas Hopko, Theodore Stylianopoulos
Joseph F. Kelly, Demetrios Constantelos
Philip Khairallah, Robert Stephanopoulos

Holy Cross Orthodox Press
50 Goddard Avenue
Brookline, Massachusetts
1979

© Copyright 1979 by Holy Cross Orthodox Press
50 Goddard Avenue
Brookline, Massachusetts 02146
All rights reserved.

ISBN 0-916586-34-0
Library of Congress Number 79-3027

Grateful acknowlegment is made to
John Carroll University
for its assistance in producing this book

Cover design by Mary Vaporis

Printed in the United States of America

CONTENTS

Foreword v

Contributors and Editor vii

God and Man in the Orthodox Church,
    by Thomas Hopko 1

Staretz Silouan: A Modern Orthodox Saint,
    by Theodore Stylianopoulos 33

The Desert Fathers as Models for the Monks of the West,
    by Joseph F. Kelly 55

The Social Ethos of the Orthodox Church,
    by Demetrios J. Constantelos 75

Is There A Future for an Eastern Rite Catholicism
in the United States,
    by Philip A. Khairallah 88

Caring for Equivalents,
    by Robert G. Stephanopoulos 95

FOREWORD

The three major divisions in the Christian Church emphasize three different aspects of the Christian Tradition. The Roman Catholic Church, proclaiming Peter as its Head, accentuates the authority of the Hierarchy; the Protestant denominations, pointing to Paul the Apostle, insist on spiritual freedom and rejection of the slavery of the Law; the Orthodox Church, more akin to John the Divine, celebrates the glory and majesty of the Lord. It is with this last Tradition that these papers deal; they highlight certain perspectives in its rich theological thought and spiritual life.

Hopefully this book will reach all the Churches. If, as the French Catholic theologian Yves Congar has said, Eastern and Western Christians drifted apart because of "estrangement and not schism," it is through renewed contact and dialogue that the estrangement may be remedied and mutual acceptance promoted. Of the six authors included in this volume, five live in the Byzantine Tradition: Father Thomas Hopko, who shares his enthusiasm for the warm, prayerful theology about God; Father Demetrios Constantelos, who illustrates how Orthodox love of God must also be love of neighbor *(philanthropia)*; Father Theodore Stylianopoulos, who allows us to savor the deep faith and simple beauty in the spiritual life of an Orthodox saint *(staretz)*; Father Robert Stephanopoulos and Father Philip Khairallah, who both speak from personal experience in the area of ecumenical projects. Doctor Joseph Kelly, a Roman Catholic, surveys Eastern influence on a type of Western spirituality, hagiography.

The first, second and fourth chapters were delivered as public addresses at John Carroll University while Fathers Hopko, Constantelos and Stylianopoulos were on campus team-teaching a course on the Orthodox Church (30 May to 16 June 1978). The entire program was sponsored by the Walter and Mary Tuohy Chair of Interreligious Studies. This chair, now in its twelfth year, is unique in the United States, bringing to the university outstanding scholars to non-Christians as well.

Father M. Edmund Hussey, a Roman Catholic, was also a participant in this year's Tuohy program. He lectured to several classes on the necessary conditions for re-establishment of the Communion of Churches in the East and West. He was unable to contribute to this volume, but many of his ideas are shared by Father Stephanopoulos who has incorporated some of them into his own paper, but, of course, from an Orthodox point of view.

It is fondly wished that these papers will reach a wide audience so that many more people than those who attended the classes and lectures may share both the learning and experience which made them possible.

John Carroll University Francis D. Costa, S. S. S.
Cleveland, Ohio

THE CONTRIBUTORS

REV. DEMETRIOS J. CONSTANTELOS is Professor of History and Religious Studies at Stockton State College. A past president of the Orthodox Theological Society of America, he has written four books on Greek Orthodoxy and Byzantine history, including *Byzantine Philanthropy and Social Welfare,* and articles for many journals such as *The Greek Orthodox Theological Review, Anglican Theological Review, Catholic Historical Review,* and *Byzantion.*

REV. THOMAS HOPKO is Assistant Professor of Systematic Theology at Saint Vladimir's Seminary. He was president of the Orthodox Theological Society of America in 1978, and his many ecumenical activities include membership on the Faith and Order Commission of the World Council of Churches. He is the author of *The Spirit of God* and has published articles in *Saint Vladimir's Theological Quarterly, Worship,* and *Diakonia.*

JOSEPH F. KELLY is Associate Professor of Religious Studies at John Carroll University. A member of the editorial board of *Theological Studies,* he has edited a volume in the *Corpus Christianorum* series and an earlier volume of Tuohy Chair papers, *Perspectives on Scripture and Tradition.* He has published articles in several journals including *Studia Patristica, Augustinian Studies, Mediaevalia,* and *Annuale Mediaevale.*

REV. PHILIP KHAIRALLAH, M.D., is a priest of the Melkite Church in the United States. He is Scientific Director and Department Head of Cardiovascular Research at the Cleveland Clinic Foundation and has written for medical publications. He is very active in ecumenical activities in the Greater Cleveland area.

REV. ROBERT STEPHANOPOULOS is pastor of Saints Constantine and Helen Church, Cleveland, and Director of the Interchurch Office of the Greek Orthodox Archdiocese. He has authored *Guidelines for Orthodox Christians in Ecumenical Relations* and articles for a variety of journals, including the *Journal of Ecumenical Studies,* and *Saint Vladimir's Seminary Quarterly.*

REV. THEODORE G. STYLIANOPOULOS is Professor of New Testament and Eastern Orthodox Spirituality at the Holy Cross Greek Orthodox School of Theology and Hellenic College. He is the author of *Justin Martyr and the Mosaic Law* and of articles in the *Greek Orthodox Theological Review, Journal of Ecumenical Studies,* and *Saint Vladimir's Seminary Quarterly.*

EDITOR, REV. FRANCIS D. COSTA, S. S. S., is Professor of Religious Studies and Chairman of the department at John Carroll University. A specialist in ecclesiology and sacramental theology, he contributed several articles to *The New Catholic Encyclopedia* and authored a 36-month homiletic feature, "The Living Word," to the journal *Emmanuel.* He is also book review editor of that journal.

GOD AND MAN IN THE ORTHODOX CHURCH
by
THOMAS HOPKO

> We have seen the true Light
> We have received the heavenly Spirit.
> We have found the true faith.
> Worshipping the Undivided Trinity
> Who has saved us.
>
> *Liturgy of Saint John Chrysostom*

Many people approach the Orthodox Church expecting what Thomas Merton once called an "excitingly mystical excursion into the realm of a very 'mystical' and highly 'spiritual' religion, a gold-encrusted cult thick with the smoke of incense and populated with a legion of gleaming icons in the sacred gloom ...."[1] In the essay in which Father Merton wrote these words, he warned the reader that when he comes to see what Orthodoxy is really about, he may perhaps be highly "disturbed."[2] I would be quick to add that he may also be not a little disappointed.

It is my purpose in the pages to follow, if not to disturb, then certainly to disappoint those looking for any sort of "sacred gloom" in their interest in Orthodoxy. It is my task to present the fundamental vision of the Orthodox Church about God and man so that the reader might see what lies beneath the smoke and the gold and the gloom which fascinate so many and serve only to distract them from what it is that Orthodox Christianity is really about.

The Knowledge of God

The fundamental affirmation of Orthodox Christianity is that God exists and that He can be known. The knowledge of God is, for the Orthodox, the only real purpose of life. Indeed, according to Orthodoxy, it is *life itself*. "And this is eternal life, that they may know Thee, the only true God, and Jesus Christ, whom Thou has sent." (John 17:3)

From its simplest parochial catechisms to the most sublime theology of its saints, and in every one of its liturgical prayers and hymns, the Orthodox Church proclaims that God is not only to be believed in, worshipped, loved and served, but that God is also to be known. Centuries ago the firm defender of Christian orthodoxy, St. Athanasios the Great, put it this way:

> For what use is existence to the creature if it cannot know its Maker? How could men be reasonable beings if they had no knowledge of the Word and Reason of the Father through whom they had received their being? They would be no better than the beasts, had they no knowledge except of earthly things; and why should God have made them at all, if He had not intended them to know Him? But, in fact, the good God has given them a share in His own image, that is, in our Lord Jesus Christ, and has made even themselves after the same Image and Likeness. Why? Simply in order that through this gift of God-likeness in themselves they may be able to perceive the Image Absolute, that is, the Word Himself, and through Him to apprehend the Father; which knowledge of their Maker is for men the only truly happy and blessed life.[3]

It is characteristic of our time to deny that God can be known in any real sense of the term *knowledge*. Not only are there many widespread and pervasive philosophical doctrines which claim that knowledge belongs only to "earthly things," to the world of the observable, the weighable and the measurable; and perhaps also to the realm of mathematical and logical forms; but there are also diverse sociological and (one might add) "political" and "psychological" positions which say that any affirmation that God can be known opens the door to religious and ecclesiastical bigotry, since it would be tantamount to affirming that in moral, theological and spiritual matters, some people are *right* and other people are *wrong*.

Even theologians can be found today, and not a few of them of the most diverse persuasions and methods, who would insist that the knowledge of God is impossible, strictly speaking. They call for a plurality of "theologies" in which there is not only a variety of human expressions, concepts, symbols and words about God, but in which there is also a clear contradiction and opposition of meanings about who and what God is, and how He acts in and toward man and the world. The plurality of theologies, even of contradictory and opposite meaning, is defended on the basis of the absolute unknowability of God in his innermost being (the *apophatic* character of God, in theological terms); the great variety of divine expressions and manifestations of God in and toward man and the world; and the immense variety of human situations and circumstances in which man claims to make assertions about the nature of God through multiform and diverse categories of expression and explanation.

While affirming that God is indeed unknowable in His innermost essence; and that there are indeed a multitude of divine manifestations and revelations of God in and toward His creatures; and that there are, as a matter of fact, an immense variety of forms and categories of expression and explanation proper to God in human thinking and speech; the Orthodox Church would remain adamant in its insistence that not all of man's thoughts and words are truly "adequate to Divinity" (in the expression of St. Gregory the Theologian of Nazianzos). Some of man's ideas and words about God are plainly wrong, being as they are, the inventions of the vain imagination of men's minds and not the fruit of a living experience of the Divine in His actual reality.

Thus, it remains the position of the Orthodox Church, however it is judged and whatever its implications and consequences, that there is truth and falsehood in theological and spiritual matters, and that theology — certainly *Christian* theology — is not a matter of taste or opinion, or speculation and erudition, or the "right philosophical premises" and the "proper logical categories"; but that theology is solely the matter of giving proper expression to the reality of God as He reveals Himself to man, "working salvation in the midst of the earth." (Psalm 74:12)

God can and must be known, the Orthodox Church claims, because God has revealed Himself to a creature capable of knowing Him. God has manifested Himself to his creatures, and not simply some data or information about Himself. He has made Himself known to men who are made in His image and according to His likeness for the express purpose of knowing Him. And the "image" and "likeness" in which man, both male and female, is created is God's own eternal and uncreated Image and Word, His only begotten Son Who exists with Himself in the exact identity of being, action and life. We have seen this point clearly affirmed in the quotation from St. Athanasios.

Man, in both its male and female forms of existence, is made in the image of God. And this image of God is a divine person. He is the Son and Word Who exists "from the beginning" with the Father, the one "by whom all things were made."[4] This is the Church's faith, the affirmation of the holy scriptures and the witness of the saints of both the Old and New Testaments. "By the Word of the Lord the heavens were made, and all their host by the Spirit of His mouth." (Psalm 33:6)

> In the beginning was the Word, and the Word was with God, and the Word was God. He was in the beginning with God; all things were made by Him, and without Him was not anything made that was made. In Him was life, and the life was the light of men. (John 1:1-3)

The scriptures and the saints bear witness that the way to the knowledge of God is not by reasoning. God cannot be known by rational operations and logical deductions, though by such methods men may come to the conviction that there must be God and that He ought to exist. God is known rather by faith, by repentance, by purity of heart and by prayer; which is to say that He is known by the spiritual attitude of openness to His self-manifestation and by the existential acknowledgment of His operations within man and the world, which acknowledgment necessarily takes the form of adoration and worship. "He who prays truly is a theologian," says the often-quoted spiritual dictum of the Orthodox Tradition, "and he is a theologian who truly prays."[5] And, in the words of St. John Climacos, "the climax of purity is the foundation of theology."[6]

> ... the climax of purity is the foundation of theology. He who has perfectly united his feelings to God is mystically led by Him to an understanding of His words. But without this union it is difficult to speak about God. The engrafted Word perfects purity, and slays death by His presence; and after slaying death, the disciple of divine knowledge is enlightened. The Word of the Lord which is from God the Father is pure, and remains so eternally. But he who has not come to know God merely speculates. Purity makes its disciple a theologian, who of himself grasps the dogmas of the Trinity.[7]

Man comes to know God when he preserves the original purity of his nature as a spiritual being stamped by the uncreated Image of God and inspired by His divine Spirit; or rather when he "rediscovers" and "uncovers" this original purity by God's gracious action through His Word and His Spirit. When man lives "according to nature," without corrupting or perverting his being made as the reflection of the perfect being of his Maker, the knowledge of God is his most natural action, his most normal possession. In his commentary on the Beatitudes, St. Gregory of Nyssa made this point in the following way:

> Now the divine nature, as it is in itself, according to its essence, transcends every act of comprehensive knowledge, and it cannot be approached or attained by our speculation. Man has never discovered a faculty to comprehend the incomprehensible; nor have we ever been able to devise an intellectual technique for grasping the inconceivable .... (Yet) it is clear that the Lord does not deceive us when He promises that the pure of heart shall see God (Matthew 5:8) .... The Lord does not say that it is blessed to know something about God, but rather to possess God in oneself: Blessed are the pure in heart, *for they shall see God*. By this I do not think He means that the man who purifies the eye of his soul will enjoy an immediate vision of God ... this teaches us that the man who purifies his heart of every creature and every passionate impulse will see the image of the divine nature in his own beauty ....

> All of you mortals ... do not despair at never being able to behold the degree of the knowledge of God which you can attain. For when God made you, He at once endowed your nature with this perfection.... You must then wash away, by a life of virtue, the dirt that came to cling to your heart like plaster, and then your divine beauty will once again shine forth....
>
> When your mind is untainted by any evil, free of passion, purified of all stain, then you will be *blessed* because your eye is clear. Then because you have been purified you will perceive things that are invisible to the unpurified.... And what is this vision? It is purity, holiness, simplicity, and other such brilliant reflections of the nature of God; for it is in these that God is seen.[8]

What St. Gregory of Nyssa says here, which is truly a common teaching of the Orthodox Church fathers, is nothing other than what the apostle Paul has written in the opening lines of his letter to the Romans:

> For the wrath of God is revealed from heaven against all ungodliness and wickedness of men who by their wickedness suppress the truth. For what can be known of God is plain to them, because God has shown it to them. Ever since the creation of the world His invisible nature, namely, His eternal power and deity, has been clearly perceived in the things that have been made. So they are without excuse, for although they knew God they did not honor him as God or give thanks to Him, but they became futile in their thinking and their senseless minds were darkened.... And since they did not see fit to acknowledge God, God gave them up to a base mind and to improper conduct. (Romans 1:18-21; 28)

The pure in heart see God everywhere; within their own nature and in everything that God has made. The pure in heart know that "the whole earth is filled with His glory." (Isaiah 6:3) The pure in heart are capable of seeing and believing, of believing and coming to *know*. It is the "fool" who "says in his heart, 'There is no God.'" And this is so because fools are "corrupt, doing abominable iniquity." This is so because they are not "wise," they are "all alike depraved," they do not "seek after God," they are "fallen away," they do not "seek after God" or "call upon God." They "work evil" and because of this, "have no understanding." (Psalm 53:1-4) The psalmist's description of the fool and the cause of his folly and ignorance of God has been summed up in the patristic tradition of the Church in the doctrine that the cause of every ignorance in man is willful rebellion against God rooted in prideful self-love. According to St. Maximos the Confessor, the very "original sin" is the "love of self" which enslaves man to the passions of the flesh and plunges him into ignorance, folly and darkness.[9] It is the love of self which produces ignorance in the willful refusal to see, to hear and to understand the words of God and God the Word Himself. For this is Jesus' own accusation against the foolishly ignorant, quoting Isaiah, when He says that they have eyes but will not see, ears but will not hear, and minds, but refuse to understand.[10]

It is urgent for us today to see this point clearly and to understand it well. The knowledge of God is given to those willing to know. The seekers will find. This is the promise of God Himself. But there are myriad reasons why men are unwilling, all of which are rooted, in one way or another, in prideful and sinful self-love, in what can only be described as impurity of heart. The scriptural teaching, witnessed by the saints, is that the impure in heart prefer their own wisdom to the wisdom of God and their own ways of behavior to the commandments of God. Some of them, according to St. Paul, have a "zeal for God" but it remains "unenlightened" because preferring a righteousness of their own making, they reject the "righteousness which comes from God." (Romans 10:3) And all of them victimize others through their propagation of ignorance which results in a culture of chaos, confusion and darkness.

The reduction of modern man to something else, and something infinitely less than the creature made in the image and likeness of God with the "command to be god by grace" (St. Basil the Great),[11] is the greatest of tragedies, the result of a culture of sin and prideful self-love. In the name of man's liberation from the gods, man has been severed from the roots of his being in the only Source and Archetype of his existence and has become enslaved, in St. Paul's words once more, to the "elements of this world."[12] We see today numberless doctrines of man which make him anything and everything from a passing and meaningless moment in some mythical historical-evolutionary process or material-economic dialectic, to the passive victim of biological, social, economic, psychological or sexual powers whose tyranny in comparison to the gods who have been conquered is incomparably more ruthless and oppressive. And the fact that theologians appear to provide their professional sanction to the tyrannous power of self-contained and self-explained "nature" only serves to add insult to the injury. But it need not be this way. And Orthodox Christianity is there to witness that indeed it is not this way. The sovereign freedom of man bestowed, preserved and guaranteed by the God whose created image man is, is still available and accessible if men will only have eyes to see, ears to hear, and a mind willing to understand.

The Knowledge of God in Christ and the Spirit

Whenever the true God is known, and men know themselves by Him, He is known through God's Son and Word, Jesus Christ, by the power of God's Holy Spirit. This is the doctrine of the scriptures and the saints. ". . . no one knows the Son except the Father, and no one knows the Father except the Son and anyone to whom the Son chooses to reveal Him." (Matthew 11:27) This means that wherever, whenever and however God is known, He is known by the agency of the Son of God, the divine Logos and Image. Even the professed atheist, or the person who has never heard of the Father or the Son, who yet has the least inkling of something good and beautiful and true, has this sense, according to the Orthodox Christian tradition, because God is with him through His Son and Word, making His nature known to him by His Holy Spirit.

God always acts towards man and the world by His Word and Spirit. The very nature of man is, as we have seen, both logical and spiritual, imprinted by God's Logos and sealed by His Spirit to be the created epiphany and reflection of Himself. According to the Bible and the Fathers, man can know and do good and reign and create because of his communion with God; and wherever and in whomever the truth is to be found, and the good and the beautiful and the wise and the noble — and any positive form of spiritual existence — this is because of God manifesting His being and action and life in His creature whom He loves. Indeed, the creation itself, the heavens and the earth, the plants and animals are all made as the created epiphanies of the Divine, the mirrors of the glory of God Who has centered His creative activities in man as the "microcosm" in whom all forms of creaturely existence are united, and the "mediator" of the whole of creation before the throne of its Maker.[13] We can hear St. Gregory of Nyssa once more speaking to us on this essential point of Christian doctrine:

> For this is the safest way to protect the good things you enjoy: by realizing how much your creator has honored you above all other creatures. He did not make the heavens in His image, nor the moon, the sun, the beauty of the stars, nor anything else which surpasses all understanding. You alone are a similitude of Eternal Beauty, and if you look at Him, you will become what He is, imitating Him who shines within you, whose glory is reflected in your purity. Nothing in all creation can equal your grandeur. All the heavens can fit in the palm of God's hand . . . and though He is so great . . . you can wholly embrace Him. He dwells within you . . . . He pervades your entire being . . . .[14]

When, because of sin and the perversion and corruption of his God-like nature through prideful self-love, man plunges himself, his children and his fellow-men into ignorance, folly and darkness, the Creator Himself acts to restore His image in His creature and to bring him once again into communion with Himself. The Creator acts, as He always acts, by His Word and His Spirit—called by St. Irenaeos the "two hands of God"—to enlighten His creature with His divine knowledge and wisdom. He acts in His self-revelation in the Law and the prophets to His chosen people, Israel. He gives them His Word and inspires them with His Spirit that they might know Him and worship Him and find life in His Name. And when the human person was found capable and worthy to fulfill the final act of God's self-manifestation to man and the world through her gracious cooperation with God's power and will, God the Word Himself became man in His own person from the holy virgin Mary, and through Him the Holy Spirit was poured out upon all flesh.

> For Thou, who art God inexpressible, existing uncreated before the ages, and ineffable, didst descend upon earth, and didst take on the semblance of a servant, and wast made in the likeness of man; for, because of the tender compassion of thy mercy, O Master, thou couldst not endure to behold mankind oppressed by the devil, but thou didst come and thou didst save us. We confess thy grace. We conceal not thy gracious acts. We proclaim thy mercy. Thou has redeemed the generation of mortal nature. By thy birth thou didst sanctify the virgin's womb. All creation magnifieth thee, who hast manifested thyself. For thou hast revealed thyself upon earth, and hast dwelt among men.[15]

This prayer taken from the Orthodox liturgy of baptism, read at the blessing of the waters, reveals the very essence of the Christian faith: "And the Word became flesh and dwelt among us, full of grace and truth..." (John 1:14) For what was God to do, says St. Athanasios again, when He "beheld man oppressed by the devil" who is in Jesus' words, the "murderer from the beginning and has nothing to do with the truth, because there is no truth in him" as "the liar and the father of lies" (John 8:44), but to "come" and "save us"?

What was God to do in face of this dehumanizing of mankind, this universal hiding of the knowledge of Himself by the wiles of the evil spirit? Was He to keep silence before so great a wrong and let men go on being thus deceived and kept in ignorance of Himself? If so, what was the use of having made them in His own Image originally?... What then was God to do? What else could He possibly do, being God, but to renew His Image in mankind, so that through it men might once more come to know Him? And how could this be done except by the coming of the very Image Himself, our Saviour Jesus Christ? . . . The Word of God came in His own Person, because it was He alone, the Image of the Father, Who could recreate man made after the Image.[16]

The Orthodox Church proclaims this central affirmation of her faith not only in the first great prayer of her baptismal liturgy, in and through which the human person is recreated, renewed and restored to his proper nature as made in the image of God; but she places this affirmation at the center of her eucharistic thanksgiving in the divine liturgy called by the name of St. Basil the Great:

> For Thou didst not turn Thyself away forever from Thy creature, whom Thou hadst made, O Good One, nor didst Thou forget the work of Thy hands. Through the tender compassion of Thy mercy, Thou didst visit him in various ways. Thou didst send prophets. Thou didst perform mighty works by Thy saints who in every generation were well-pleasing to Thee. Thou didst speak to us by the mouth of Thy servants, the prophets, foretelling to us the salvation which was to come. Thou didst give us the law as a help. Thou didst appoint angels as guardians. And when the fullness of time had come, Thou didst speak to us through Thy Son Himself, by whom Thou didst create the ages; who, being the Radiance of Thy Glory and Image of Thy Person, upholding all things by the word of His power, thought it not robbery to be equal to Thee, the God and Father. He was God before the ages, yet He appeared on earth and lived among men, becoming incarnate of the holy virgin . . . He emptied Himself, taking the form of a servant, being likened to the body of our lowliness that He might liken us to the image of His Glory . . . .[17]

What the holy Church prays is what the scripture teaches. Jesus Christ, the Logos incarnate, has come to deliver man from demonic delusion and darkness, to liberate him from his enslavement to the culture and tradition of confusion and sin, and to transfer him once again into the kingdom of divine wisdom, insight and light. The scriptures, especially the writings of St. John and St. Paul, repeat this message over and again. The Wisdom and Word of God has come to the world in human form, in human flesh, and in Him "are hid all the treasures of wisdom and knowledge" and the "whole fullness of deity bodily" so that in him man might "put off the old nature with its practices" and "put on the new nature which is being renewed in knowledge after the image of the Creator." (Colossians 2:3-10; 3:9)

Jesus Christ renews the nature of man by sanctifying and sealing it with the Spirit of God. It is by the Holy Spirit, the Spirit of Truth who proceeds from the Father and is sent into the world through the Son, that human beings come to know God and to address Him with His most exalted name of Abba, Father.[18] For the Holy Spirit takes what is Christ's and declares it to men, bringing to remembrance all that Jesus has said and done, and guiding men into all truth.[19] A modern Orthodox writer, the Elder Silouan (Silvanus) who died on Mount Athos in 1938, wrote this way about the knowledge of God by the Holy Spirit:

> The Lord is made known in the Holy Spirit, and the Holy Spirit pervades the entire man: soul, mind and body. In this way God is known in heaven and on earth.
>
> If you would know the Lord's love for us, hate sin and wrong thoughts, and day and night pray fervently. The Lord will then give you His grace, and you will know Him through the Holy Spirit, and after death, when you enter into paradise, there too you will know Him through the Holy Spirit, as you knew Him on earth.
>
> We do not need riches or learning to know the Lord. We must simply be obedient and sober, have a humble spirit and love our fellow-men.
>
> We may study as much as we will, but we shall still not come to know the Lord unless we live according to His commandments for the Lord is not made known through learning, but by the Holy Spirit. Many philosophers and scholars have arrived at a belief in the existence of God, but they have not come to know Him. To believe in God is one thing, to know God is another. Both in heaven and on earth the Lord is made known only by the Holy Spirit, and not through ordinary learning.

Now the saints declare that they have seen God; yet there are people who say that God is not. No doubt they say this inasmuch as they have not known God, but it does not at all mean that He is not. The saints speak of that which they have actually seen, of that which they know .... Even the souls of the heathen sensed that God is, though they were ignorant how to worship the true God. But the Holy Spirit instructed the prophets of old and after them the apostles and then our holy fathers and bishops, and in this way the true faith came down to us. And we knew the Lord by the Holy Spirit, and when we knew Him our souls were confirmed in Him.[20]

This doctrine of the peasant monk of our day might appear as the anti-intellectual, anti-theological pietism of a man justifying his lack of education and learning, and his separation from the worldly sciences of man, by the mindless appeal to charismatic devotion and mystical illumination. But it is the doctrine of the apostle to the gentiles, whom no one can accuse of lacking erudition. And it is the doctrine as well of the greatest of theologians and intellectuals found in the Christian Tradition; men and women schooled in philosophy, literature and all of the human and natural sciences of their day.[21]

The doctrine of Silouan, which is really that of the scriptures, especially the writings of Saint John, may also be taken simply as a radically individualistic teaching which can in no way be cast in objective terms. It would certainly be considered by many so-called theologians today as mere piety and prophecy, and not at all as *theology* since it is considered to be totally devoid of scientific verification, lacking — as it is taken to be — in any kind of concrete, historical, suprapersonal, corporate, institutional and objectively-existing expressions and forms. The appreciation of Silouan's writings by the Orthodox, however, would be that he gives voice to a personal experience which is only possible if there exists a corporate community within the time and space of this world which allows for man to have such an experience, and gives that identical experience to all persons who enter into the reality of its life. For the Orthodox Christian this objectively-existing community exists; it is called the holy Church.

The Knowledge of God in the Church

The Christian Church, according to the Orthodox Faith, is God's new covenant with man; the final and everlasting covenant of peace which He makes with man in the person of His Son, the Messiah of Israel and the Saviour of the world.

> Behold, the days are coming, says the Lord, when I will make a new covenant . . . not like the covenant which I made with their fathers . . . my covenant which they broke, though I was their husband, says the Lord. But this is the covenant which I will make with the house of Israel after those days, says the Lord. I will put my law within them and I will write it upon their hearts; and I will be their God, and they shall be my people. And no longer shall each man teach his neighbor and teach his brother, saying, "Know the Lord," for they shall all know me, from the least of them to the greatest, says the Lord. For I will forgive them their iniquity and I will remember their sin no more. (Jeremiah 31:31-34)

In the new covenant which God makes with His people in Christ, He teaches them Himself by putting a "new spirit" within them, which is His own Spirit, the Spirit of God.[22] In the Orthodox Tradition, the Church herself is defined as "life in the Holy Spirit" and the "Kingdom of God on earth" not in any purely "interior" and "mystical" way in the hidden life of the soul, but concretely and objectively in the sacramental and doctrinal life of the covenant community which is incarnate in space and time, lives in this present age, and is locatable in human history. The well-known Russian Orthodox emigré theologian, Father Sergius Bulgakov, put it this way in the opening words of his book *The Orthodox Church*:

> Orthodoxy is the Church of Christ on earth. The Church of Christ is not an institution; it is new life with Christ and in Christ, guided by the Holy Spirit. Christ, the Son of God, came to earth, was made man, uniting His divine life with that of humanity.
>
> The Church, in her quality of Body of Christ, which lives with the life of Christ, is by that fact the domain where the Holy Spirit lives and works. More: the Church is life by the

Holy Spirit because it is the body of Christ. This is why the Church may be considered as a blessed life in the Holy Spirit, or the life of the Holy Spirit in humanity.[23]

This is also why St. Cyprian of Carthage could write centuries earlier that "he is not a Christian who is not in the Church of Christ" and "he cannot have God as Father who has not the Church as Mother" and, most bluntly, "without the Church there is no salvation." For as Father Georges Florovsky has said, commenting on the text which he labelled a tautology, *"Salvation is the Church."*[24]

Salvation is the Church, and the Church is salvation; the gift of eternal life in the knowledge of God through communion with Him in His Son and His Spirit. This is the Orthodox Faith. The Lord God Almighty acts in the world by His Word and His Spirit, and He does so always through the community He gathers. God always acts toward man as a whole. In the dispensation of salvation which is the restoration of man's nature and the whole of creation begun in the Old Covenant and fulfilled in Christ's Church, God reveals Himself to a body of believers. God does not act toward isolated individuals. He does not reveal Himself to men in the privacy of their souls. He deals with communities, the covenant communities and the whole of mankind. If we ask the reason for this, the traditional Orthodox answer would be that God simply cannot act towards individuals in isolation because there simply is no such thing as an "isolated individual."

The "isolated individual" is the product of man's fallen imagination. It is a product of sin. Such a reality simply does not exist; it is no reality at all. What does exist are persons in community: men living together in the world in an identity of nature which cannot be broken except at the cost of man's perversion of reality and his destruction of himself. What God has taught us in the manifestation of His Word is that we are of necessity "members one of another." (Ephesians 4:25) It is interesting to note how even St. Anthony the Great, the father of monks known for his seclusion in solitary confinement, has repeated this teaching in each of his letters:

And He has gathered us out of all lands by the Word of His power, from one end of the earth to the other end of the world, and made resurrection of our minds (and our hearts), and remission of our sins, and taught us that we are members one of another.[25]

Man alone is not man. This is the teaching; just as God alone is not God. The doctrine of the Holy Trinity at this point is of crucial significance.

We have indicated already how, according to the scriptures and the saints, God Himself would not be God if He were without His personal Son and His Spirit; and how the witness of the bible and the tradition of the Church is consistent in its insistence that God Almighty has an only-begotten Son and a most Holy Spirit in His very being as God. The eternal generation of the Son and Word of God — His uncreated Image — and the eternal procession from the Father to the life-creating Spirit belong to God's being as God. If we seek a reason for this, the traditional response of the saints would be that the God who is Love, the God who is Good, the God who is living and active by nature, could not possibly be God if He were alone in His divinity. He would not and could not be God if He were not an essentially self-communicating, self-sharing, self-manifesting being. A God without an *eternal* self-expression in the most perfect divine form would just not be God and could not possibly be understood in any sense of the terms as Goodness and Love. In more traditional words, a God without a personal divine Son and a personal Holy Spirit is not only not the God of the Bible known by the saints and glorified in the Church, but He would not be a God in any way logically and theologically comprehensible, living and acting as Goodness and Love. This means that multi-personality belongs to divine being and life as an absolute necessity. A uni-personal God is no God at all. He is the figment, once again, of man's fallen imagination, a creation of creatures. A God devoid of a personal Son, Word and Image, and a personal divine Spirit would be monstrous, according to the saints. He would be, if He were this way, the eternal prototype of self-containment, self-sufficiency, self-isolation and self-adoration. He would be the metaphysical archetype of the self-centered individual and not of the self-sharing person who exists in community with others in the union of love, being, and life. As St. Gregory the Theologian put it in the fourth century in defending his "beloved Trinity" against the attacks of the philosophers with their alleged perfect Absolute Monad: Our God is "enosis," not simply "en." He is *communion*, not simply *one*. And *communion* is far superior to mere oneness, for it is perfect unity without suppression of diversity; and perfect diversity without the destruction of unity.[26]

God is, in this vision, not the supreme individual. He is the perfect Person in communion with Divine Persons Who are other than Himself; yet in absolute union and unity of being, action and life. God is the Father, the source of divinity; with the only-begotten Son and Word, born of the Father in the timeless generation; and the "holy, good and life-creating Spirit" (to use the traditional Orthodox doxological expression), Who proceeds from the Father and abides in the Son; as St. John Damascene has said it: The Most Holy Trinity, one in essence and undivided.

The Orthodox Church gives glory and honor to the Tri-Personal God in this way, as the following hymn from the Vespers of Pentecost bears witness:

> Come, let us worship the Tri-Personal Godhead,
> The Son in the Father with the Holy Spirit.
> The Father timelessly begets the co-reigning
>   and co-eternal Son,
> The Holy Spirit was in the Father, glorified
>   equally together with the Son.
> One Power. One Essence. One Divinity.
> In worshipping Him, let us say:
> Holy God, Who made all things through the Son,
>   with the cooperation of the Holy Spirit.
> Holy Mighty, through whom we know the Father
>   and by whom the Holy Spirit came into the world.
> Holy Immortal, the Comforting Spirit, proceeding
>   from the Father and resting in the Son.
> O Holy Trinity! Glory to Thee![27]

Mankind is made to reflect the Holy Trinity: a plurality of human persons in the unity of one and the same identical human nature. And the Church is the restoration of human nature and the recreation of creation. This is the way that St. Gregory of Nyssa has said it:

> The establishment of the Church is the recreation of the world. In the Church there is a new heaven ... here too is a new firmament ... a new earth is formed .... Man is created once again, for by his rebirth from on high he is renewed according to the image of his Creator .... And there are many stars rising on the firmament of faith. And there should be no wonder that there are many stars numbered by God in this world and called by name, for their names, says their Creator, have been written in heaven. For it is in this sense that I understood the Creator of the new universe to say to His luminaries: *Your names are written in heaven.* (Luke 10:20) This is not the only striking thing about the new creation ... there are also a multitude of suns that light up the world with the rays of good works. For thus does their Creator speak: *Let your light shine before men* (Matthew 5:16) and again: *Then shall the just shine as the sun.* (Matthew 14:43) ... So too, anyone who looks upon the universe of this new creation reflected in the Church can see in it Him Who is all in all, and ... be led by our faith into an awareness of the Transcendent. And so ... (the soul) shows how the whole Church is but the one Body of her Spouse (that is, Christ); and in her description of His beauty she attributes a particular meaning to each one of His members, but it is only by the union of all of the particular members that the beauty of the Body is complete.[28]

The Church is the "new creation." St. Paul said it first. It is the unity of many persons, graced by the Holy Spirit, in the one Body of Christ.[29] It is the experience already now, in the present age, in time and in space, of the eternal life of the Kingdom of God in the "new heaven" and "new earth" foretold by the prophets, fulfilled in Christ and the Spirit, and seen in the mystic vision of St. John the Theologian. And the Church is not only newness. It is also fullness. It is the participation in the new humanity of Jesus, the incarnate Logos, in whom dwells the "whole fullness of deity bodily" and in whom man has come to "fullness of life." "And of His fullness have we all received, grace upon grace." (John 1:16) It is the Church which is Christ's Body, "the fullness of Him Who fills all in all." (Ephesians 1:23)

> He is the head of the body, the Church; he is the beginning, the first-born from the dead, that in everything he might be pre-eminent. For in him all the fulness of God was pleased to dwell, and through him to unite all things, whether on earth or in heaven . . . . (Colossians 1:18-20)

> For he has made known to us in all wisdom and insight the mystery of his will, according to his purpose which he set forth in Christ as a plan for the fulness of time, to unite all things in him, things in heaven and things on earth . . . and he has put all things under his feet and has made him the head over all things for the Church, which is his body, the fulness of him who fills all in all. (Ephesians 1:9-10, 22-23)

There is an urgent need today for people to rediscover the Church. There is a critical need to go beyond all the rhetoric about theologies and traditions, beyond all claims about the contributions and enrichments of the many sects and denominations and to discover again the reality of the "household of God, which is the Church of the living God, the pillar and bulwark of the truth." (I Timothy 3:15)

God has established his final and everlasting covenant with men in the Messiah. What the prophets have predicted has come to pass. The covenant in the blood of the Son of God, the living temple animated by the Spirit of God, is with us. The virgin has conceived and borne a child. Jesus Christ has come and established His Church and "the gates of hell shall not (and indeed cannot) prevail against it." (Matthew 16:18)

The Church of the living God exists on earth. It is not some invisible ideal far off in the heavens. Neither is it a conglomeration of competing and contradicting denominations and sects. Nor is it a charismatic fellowship of believers singing of their unity in the Spirit, despite all evidence to the contrary. Nor is it a company of confessional families, each one confessing in its own peculiar way. Nor is it some sort of divinely established organization ruled on earth by sacerdotal potentates serving up infallible decrees and moral pronouncements for the spiritual benefit of its subjects. It is the Church of the living God: Christ and His Body. Christ and His Bride. The True Vine and His branches. The Chief Cornerstone and His living stones built into an animated temple in the sovereign freedom of the Spirit of God. The Great Highpriest with Himself as the blameless offering, offering in Himself the whole of creation to the Father. It is the King of the Kingdom of God, with those who reign with Him. The Good Pastor with His sheep. The Master with His disciples. God with man and man with God in the communion of truth and love, in the unity of being and life, in the glorious freedom of the Most Holy Trinity.

The Church of the living God is a sacramental community. It exists as an objective, historical reality in the midst of the earth. It is one Church, with the unity of God. It is the holy Church, with the holiness of its Thrice-Holy Lord. It is the catholic Church, with the limitless fullness of the boundless nature of the Godhead. It is the apostolic Church, sent into the world with the mission of its Master committed and entrusted to His apostles and their successors in the body. It is simply *salvation.*

There is a gracious humanity to the Church. It could not be otherwise, for it is humans who are being saved. But the humanity of the Church is not a "mere humanity." It is certainly not a "sinful humanity." It is the divine humanity of the God-man Christ. It is man's original humanity made divine by the grace of the Holy Spirit. It is into this humanity, restored, resurrected, renewed and recreated that a person is born on the day of his baptism.

A person enters the Church by dying and rising with Christ in the sacrament of baptism which is called in the Orthodox Tradition by the name of "holy illumination." The baptismal font, St. Cyril of Jerusalem reminds us, is the tomb and the womb, the grave and the mother.[30] The person dies in the baptismal waters with Christ to be born anew in the new humanity of the Kingdom of God. The person dies to the demon-riddled and deathbound life of this age in order to be able to live already now the eternal life of the age to come. Immediately following baptism, accomplished in the Orthodox Church by triple immersion in the name of the Trinity, the person is clothed with the white robe of salvation and receives, through the anointing with holy chrism, the "seal of the gift of the Holy Spirit."[31] This is the person's personal Pentecost, as baptism is his personal Easter. The person receives God's Spirit as a gift in order to be capable of living the life of God into which he is born in the baptismal waters. Immediately following the sacrament of chrismation (understood so differently from the great majority of Western theologies of confirmation) the newly-enlightened is led to the eucharistic table, including the infants who are baptized and chrismated, to partake of the Bread of Life, the Body and Blood of Christ, in the Marriage Supper of the Lamb in the Kingdom of God.

In the Orthodox Tradition, the Church herself, as we have seen, is called the Kingdom of God on earth. She is the Kingdom of God because she is Christ's Bride whose life consists in participation in the very nature of God which is experienced by men as the "righteousness and the peace and the joy of the Holy Spirit." (Romans 14:17)

> His divine power has granted to us all things that pertain to life and godliness, through the knowledge of Him who called us to His own glory and excellence, by which He has granted to us His precious and very great promises, that through these you may escape from the corruption that is in the world because of passion, and become partakers of the divine nature. (II Peter 1:3-4)

In the Church of Christ man enters paradise and becomes a partaker of the nature of God. The divine Liturgy of the Church, which is the Church's only formal expression as a sacramental reality, is salvation itself. It is salvation because it is communion with God and all things in Him, "things in heaven and things on earth."[32] In the Church man participates in the divine liturgy of the Most Holy Trinity, the "common action" of the Three Divine Persons. (Liturgy, as a word, means common action.) He joins with the angels in the celestial liturgy of the bodiless hosts, entering into their ceaseless singing of the Thrice-Holy Hymn to the Creator. He joins with the whole of creation in its cosmic liturgy, participating with the heavens and the earth and all of the creatures in "blessing the Lord" and "proclaiming the glory of God."[33] He comes to a reality incomparably more fearful and glorious than that "terrifying sight" which caused Moses to say, "I tremble with fear."

> But you have come to Mount Zion and to the city of the living God, the heavenly Jerusalem, and to innumerable angels in festal gathering, and the assembly (literally, *church*) of the first-born who are enrolled in heaven, and to a judge who is God of all, and to the spirits of just men made perfect, and to Jesus, the mediator of a new covenant, and to the sprinkled blood that speaks more graciously than the blood of Abel .... Therefore let us be grateful for receiving a kingdom which cannot be shaken, and thus let us offer to God acceptable worship, with reverence and awe, for our God is a consuming fire. (Hebrews 12:22-28)

This, after all, is what Thomas Merton's "gold-encrusted cult thick with the smoke of incense and populated with a legion of gleaming icons" is all about. It manifests the fact that God is with us and we are with him, with all of the angels and saints and the whole of creation in a "kingdom which cannot be shaken." Everything in the Church, not only the icons and the incense, but the songs and the hymns, the dogmas and the prayers, the vestments and the candles, the processions and the prostrations ... everything bears witness to the fact that the Church is *salvation*: communion with God in His redeemed, resurrected, transfigured and glorified creation. Everything proclaims the fact that the Messiah has come, that God is with us, and that all things have been made new. Everything cries out with the fact that "through him we have access in one Spirit to the Father" and are "no longer strangers and sojourners, but ... fellow citizens with the saints and members of the household of God ... Christ Jesus Himself being the cornerstone, in whom the whole structure is joined together, and grows into a holy temple in the Lord ... a dwelling place of God in the Spirit." (Ephesians 2:18-22)

In the divine liturgy of the Church we see why the world was created. We see God and man as they are meant to be seen. We have the vision vouchsafed to St. John the Theologian in the *Book of Revelation*. And more than vision; we have the living experience. We have *salvation*.

There are many theories about salvation abounding today. Some of them are cast in individualistic terms and have to do with men's "souls." Others of them are collectivistic and have to do with "history" or "society" or the "cosmos" or the "process." Virtually all of them position a radical dichotomy between this world and the age to come. And virtually none of them see the Church as God's good world experienced and known as the Kingdom of God.

All too often the world is defined (even by theologians) as an end in itself; either a "dead end" to be rejected and scorned, or a glorious end to be affirmed in its fallenness as all that we have. And all too often the kingdom to come is described as a reality totally alien to the life of this world; a reality scorned and rejected by some as "pie in the sky" or a reality adored by others as the radical antithesis to this "vale of tears." But in the Church of Christ such a dichotomy is impossible, and it is most happily overcome.

According to the Bible and the liturgy of the Church, God made the world and He called it "very good." (Genesis 1:31) God loves the world which He made and He does everything to save it when it is corrupted by His creatures. We have seen how the Church "prays" this affirmation in the text from the Liturgy of St. Basil the Great. God saves the world which He loves as the Bride of His Son through the incarnation of His Son who becomes what His beloved has become — which is cursed, "sin" and dead, in order to purify and renew her, and to take her once more to the home of His Father. Being the one not only "by whom" but "in whom" and "for whom all things were created" (Colossians 1:16), the Son of God becomes man, and not only man but a slave, and not only a slave but dead, and not only dead, but dead on a cross . . . in order that He might rise from the dead and ascend into the heavens to the right hand of the Father, where He is, we might be also as His Body and His Bride.[34]

For God so loved the world that He gave His only-begotten Son, that whoever believes in Him should not perish but have everlasting life. For God sent His Son into the world, not to condemn the world, but that the world through Him might be saved. (John 3:16-17)

God neither affirms and blesses the world in its rebellion and corruption, nor does He scorn and reject it. He saves it. And the Church is *salvation*: this world saved by the death and resurrection of its Maker, its Lover and its Lord; this world saved by the indwelling of God's Spirit Who allows men to experience it as the Kingdom of God, the Kingdom yet to come, known by the faithful who are willing to see, to hear and to understand what God is revealing.

What no eye has seen, nor ear heard, nor the heart of man conceived, what God has prepared for those who love Him (Isaiah 64:4), God has revealed to us through the Spirit. (I Corinthians 2:9-10)

The issue of the Church is a key issue of our time. One might even be tempted to say that it is the most important issue facing Christians today. It is the issue, the resolution of which will decide the fate not only of Christians and Christianity, but of creation itself. The choice is between a Christianity of substance and power, a Christianity of objective and universal meaning and truth, and a Christianity of taste and opinion, of subjective assertion and scholarly disputation. The choice is between a Christianity of Christ and the Church, or a Christianity construed as only one of the religions of man (perhaps the best and the highest), yet only one of the possible "spiritual experiences" open to humans, in a variety of contradictory versions and forms.

A modern author has written (I believe it was Chesterton) that when man ceases to believe in the true God, and so in His Church, he believes not in *nothing*; he believes rather in *anything*. And how many "anythings" are with us today, not a few of which are presenting themselves under the guise of Christianity. It is my firm conviction that the conversion of Christianity from the objective reality of the life and teaching of the historical Church into a great variety of the many "anythings" in which men may now believe is the greatest of tragedies. It began, the Orthodox theologians tell us, by a distortion within the ranks of the vision of God, a distortion produced by theologies born not out of the living experience of the life of God in the Church, but from the imagination of men's minds; which theologies in turn produced a distortion in the life of the Church in some of her communities, and has led us into the present confusion and darkness in which we now find ourselves wandering.

A distorted vision of God produces a distorted experience in the Church, and a distorted experience in the Church reproduces a distorted vision of God. And a distorted vision of God produces a legion of distorted images of man. And we find ourselves today with a legion of doctrines about man, some of them certainly rooted in the Christian past, but now violently opposed to the Christian vision of reality, and others claiming to be Christian while opposed to each other in their most fundamental assertions. There are those who would consecrate the great variety and diversity of Christian theologies and spiritualities which abound today, including the various definitions and experiences of what the Christian Church is, with reference to catholicity and Pentecost. But it would certainly be the conviction of the Orthodox that the more proper reference is rather to confusion and Babel. And on this point there is a liturgical reference which seems singularly pertinent. It comes from the feast of Pentecost itself:

> When the Most High came down and confused the tongues, He divided the nations; but when He distributed tongues of fire, He called all men to unity. Therefore, with one voice we glorify the All-Holy Spirit. (Kontakion of Pentecost)

The Spiritual Life

For the Orthodox Christian there is no spiritual life without the Church, since the spiritual life of a person is the existential application and actualization of the divine life which is known and experienced in the Church. Without the Church there is not only no *salvation* — there is no *spirituality* either.

Our time is one in which many people are interested in "spirituality." If we knew history better, we might have predicted it. There seems to be a pattern. After a period of rampant secularism, a season of civil strife, a time of exhausting the physical senses in hope of gratifying (ultimately without satisfaction) the carnal passions, there inevitably follows a time of religious revivalism and a season of interest in things of the spirit. After the secularism of the sixties comes the spiritualism of the seventies; and the Orthodox Christian, on the basis of past history, might well wonder which of the two is more welcome, especially in an age when Christ and the Holy Spirit are separated from the Church experienced as a sacramental reality with its liturgy, scriptures, dogmas, canons and saints.

Spirituality and spiritual life outside and without the objective reality of the Church is considered by the Orthodox as an enterprise destined to frustration and failure. It can only be a fragmented and distorted experience of life, a mixture of many things, some of darkness and some of light, unable ultimately to handle and to satisfy the whole of man's experiences with his thoughts and desires. Spiritual life without the Church, even when men take the Bible for their guide, is condemned to be an unwholesome and unfulfilling affair. It can hardly fail to be the experience of being "tossed to and fro and carried about by every wind of doctrine, by the cunning of men, by their craftiness in deceitful wiles." (Ephesians 4:14)

To make such an assertion is not at all to contend that the millions of human beings outside the communion of the Church are devoid of God's grace or are automatically shut out of the kingdom to come. God's grace surely extends beyond the earthly boundaries of the Church. This is an Orthodox dogma. The Spirit of God "blows where He wills." (John 3:8) And Jesus Christ is the Lord of the universe, the God of all people, the Logos of God in whose image every person is made. He is the Master, as well, of both evil and good; of darkness as well as light. And He works as He can, through His indwelling Spirit, with every human being, desiring as He does that "all men be saved and come to the knowledge of the truth." (I Timothy 2:4)

It is a dogma of the Orthodox Church as well that mere membership in the Church is no guarantee of salvation. The Church is salvation, but a person may participate in her saving life unto condemnation and judgment. This happens, according to the Faith, when a person participates in the life of the Church sacramentally, but as a matter of fact does not live the life of grace which God gives to His people.[35] It is even the case that persons who continue to go through the motions of churchly life, who continue to pray and participate in the sacraments, who continue to speak and give lip service to the Lord without actually surrendering themselves wholly to His will, do become worse because of these actions. They will become angry, bitter, resentful, judgmental and spiritually destroyed. "It is a fearful thing to fall into the hands of the living God" for our God is indeed a "consuming fire." (Hebrews 10:31; 12:29)

The spiritual life, according to Orthodoxy, is the personal acquisition and realization of that which is given sacramentally in the life of the Church. It is the personal "doing" of what is "done" in the Church in her liturgical life; what is prayed and proclaimed. It is the "being" at every moment, in every circumstance of what the Church herself is as Christ's Body and Bride, in her mystical and sacramental nature and form. It is, in a word, the ascetic effort, made possible by grace, of the continual glorification of God by dying and rising with Christ, in the taking of the cross, by bringing the fullness of God's kingdom to the smallest detail of everyday life; and, in turn, of raising every smallest detail of life, every thought, word and deed, into the fullness of the Kingdom of God. It is, in the words of one of my teachers, the "transformation of the routine into paradise," an expression which certainly has its source in the spiritual tradition of Orthodoxy as it is described and explained by such spiritual masters as St. Symeon the New Theologian.

No one in the Orthodox calendar of saints is more "charismatic" or "mystical" than St. Symeon the New Theologian. The following passage from his spiritual directions is characteristic (to refer once again to Thomas Merton's formula) of Orthodoxy as a "very 'mystical' and highly 'spiritual' religion":

> The only thing that God demands of us mortals is that we do not sin . . . this is merely keeping inviolate the image and high rank we possess by nature. Clothed thus in the radiant garments of the Spirit, we abide in God and He in us. Through

> grace we become gods and sons of God and are illuminated by the light of His knowledge....
>
> It is right that we should first of all bend our necks to the yoke of Christ's commandments... walking in them and zealously even unto death renewing ourselves forever and making of ourselves a fresh paradise of God until, through the Holy Spirit, the Son and the Father enter into us and dwell in us.
>
> Let us look then how to glorify God. The only way we can glorify Him is as the Son has glorified Him.... But by that, by which the Son has glorified His Father, was the Son Himself glorified by the Father. Let us then strive to do what the Son has done....
>
> This is the Cross — to become dead to the whole world; to suffer sorrows, temptations, and other passions of Christ. In bearing this cross with complete patience, we imitate Christ's passion and thus glorify our God the Father as his sons in grace, co-heirs of Christ.[36]

This is the traditional "spirituality" of the Orthodox Church. This is the way through which God is known and glorified, the way through which man finds life and fulfills himself as God's creature. It is the way of self-emptying love. It is the way ultimately of suffering.

Orthodox spirituality is the spirituality of suffering, or rather, more accurately, of co-suffering love. This is the way in which man is made perfect. It is the way in which Christ Himself, the divine Son of God, was perfected in His humanity.

> But we see Jesus... crowned with glory and honor because of the suffering of death, so that by grace of God he might taste death for every one. For it was fitting that he... should make the pioneer of their salvation perfect through suffering.... Although he was a Son, he learned obedience through what he suffered; and being made perfect he became the source of eternal salvation to all who obey him. (Hebrews 2:10; 5:7)

If we ask why it is that Jesus Himself, and all of us with Him, are "made perfect through suffering," the only answer can be that Love is perfection; and Love in the fallen world is inevitably wedded to suffering. This, too, is the reason why it is simply a matter of fact, according to Christian Orthodoxy, that a human being finds himself by losing himself, fulfills himself by emptying himself, discovers himself by forgetting himself. This is why one can only be free by being everyone's slave, rich by becoming poor, powerful by becoming meek. This is why, finally, a human person only finds life when he is willing and able to die, for death in "this world" is the perfection of giving, and *giving* belongs eternally to God as His very nature and life.

We reflected above on the fact that God Almighty is an essentially self-sharing being. We saw how, according to Orthodox doctrine, a God who would be enclosed in His own individual existence could not be the God Who is Love. It is this essential self-sharing of God that is manifested in all its majesty and glory in Christ on the cross. And it is this self-sharing of Jesus, in the humanity which the Son of God has assumed "for us men and for our salvation," that makes his humanity perfect and the source of salvation for all. There is no "tragedy" in the eternal self-sharing of God in His Trinitarian being and life. And there will be no "tragedy" in the self-sharing of love which is the content of life in the Kingdom of God. But in "this world" which is fallen, whose "prince" is the devil, the perfection of love is always a cross; a terrible tragedy that is transformed into victory and glory in the person of Christ.

The content of eternal life and perfection in this present age, (and so, the content of Orthodox spirituality) is co-crucifixion with Christ in co-suffering love. This is the meaning of Jesus' "new commandment" that men should love one another even as He Himself has loved us. This is not simply the commandment of love, for that is the "old commandment" which we have had "from the beginning." This is the new commandment to love with Christ's love, which is the love of the Father poured into our hearts by the Spirit of God.

> ... and we rejoice in our hope of sharing the glory of God. More than that, we rejoice in our sufferings, knowing that that suffering produces endurance, and endurance produces character, and character produces hope, and hope does not disappoint us, because God's love has been poured into our

hearts through the Holy Spirit who has been given to us. (Romans 5:2-5)

The one, true and living God is the God Who is Love and being Love He suffers with us and for us. Man is made in the image and likeness of this God Who is Love, Whose uncreated Image and Expression is His Son Jesus Christ. The perfection of man, and the source and content and goal of his spiritual life, is to partake of God's nature and to share in His life. And that means, in this life, to share in His sufferings. The vision both of God and of man is thereby perfected in the sufferings and death of Him who comes down from heaven to become all that we are, that we might become by His Spirit all that He is. The vision is fulfilled on the Cross.

The saying is sure:
If we have died with him, we shall also live with him;
If we endure, we shall also reign with him;
If we deny him, he will deny us;
If we are faithless, he remains faithful —
For He cannot deny Himself!

(II Timothy 2:11-13)

NOTES

1. Thomas Merton, "Orthodoxy and the World," *Monastic Studies* 4 (1966), 106.

2. Ibid.

3. St. Athanasios, *On the Incarnation* (Crestwood, N.Y., 1965), p. 38.

4. See John 1.1-3, Colossians 1.16, Hebrews 1.2.

5. The source of the saying is most likely Evagrios of Pontos. It is listed in an English translation of the sayings from the Philokalia under the name of St. Nilos of Sinai; St. Nilos of Sinai, "153 Texts on Prayer," No. 61 in *Early Fathers from the Philokalia,* ed. Kadloubovsky and Palmer (London, 1954), p. 134. At a Congress of Orthodox Theological Schools held in Athens in August of 1976, no fewer than four speakers quoted this text.

6. See G. Florovsky, "The Ethos of the Orthodox Church," in *Orthodoxy, A Faith and Order Dialogue,* Faith and Order Paper No. 30 (Geneva, 1960), p. 41.

7. St. John Climacos, *The Ladder of Divine Ascent,* trans. Lazarus Moore (London, 1959), p. 264.

8. St. Gregory of Nyssa, *On the Beatitudes,* Homily 6, Patrologia Graeca 44, 1268B-1272C. See Jean Daniélou and Herbert Musurillo, *From Glory to Glory, Texts from St. Gregory of Nyssa's Mystical Writings* (New York, 1961), pp. 98-102.

9. See Lars Thunberg, *Microcosm and Mediator: The Theological Anthropology of Maximos the Confessor* (Lund, 1965), pp. 164-71, 327-42.

10. Isaiah 6.9-10; Matthew 13.14-17.

11. See Vladimir Lossky, *The Mystical Theology of the Eastern Church* (Crestwood, N.Y., 1976), p. 127.

12. Colossians 2.8, 20; Galatians 4.3.

13. See Thunberg, *Microcosm and Mediator.*

14. St. Gregory of Nyssa, *On the Canticle of Canticles,* PG 44; 804A-808B. See Daniélou and Musurillo, *From Glory to Glory,* pp. 162-63.

15. *Service Book of the Holy Orthodox-Catholic Apostolic Church,* trans. I. Hapgood (Brooklyn, N.Y., 1956), p. 278.

16. St. Athanasios, *On the Incarnation,* p. 41.

17. *The Divine Liturgy,* Official Translation of the Orthodox Church in America, 2nd. ed. (South Canaan, Pa., 1961), pp. 130-31.

18. John 14.26, 15.26, 16.13; Romans 8.15; Galatians 4.6.

19. John 14.26, 16.12-15.

20. Archimandrite Sofrony, *The Undistorted Image, Staretz Silouan: 1866-1938,* trans. Rosemary Edmonds (London, 1958), pp. 115-18. This book, now out of print, was recently published in two separate volumes by St. Vladimir's Seminary Press under the titles *The Monk of Mount Athos* and *Wisdom from Mount Athos.*

21. The Cappadocian Fathers, Basil and his brother Gregory of Nyssa and his friend Gregory of Nazianzos the Theologian, as well as John Chrysostom, John of Damascus and Gregory Palamas were certainly educated in secular disciplines, yet their doctrine is that of the Elder Silouan. In our own time such men as Florovsky, Lossky, Bulgakov, Florensky, Verhovskoy, Schmemann and Meyendorff are all academically educated and not a few of them came to theology only after passing through philosophical, literary and scientific studies. Yet they teach the doctrine of the peasant monk from Mount Athos. The well-known spiritual writer Archbishop Anthony Bloom, the Metropolitan of Sorouzh, living in London as the leader of the Russian Orthodox Church there, is still a practicing physician.

22. In addition to Jeremiah 31, see Ezekiel 36.26-27; Psalm 51.10-12; Joel 2; Isaiah 42, *et al.*

23. Sergius Bulgakov, *The Orthodox Church* (Maitland, Fla., 1935), pp. 9-10.

24. St. Cyprian of Carthage, *Letters 55* and *73,* and *On the Unity of the Catholic Church,* cited by Georges Florovsky, "Sobornost: The Catholicity of the Church," in *The Church of God,* edited by E. Mascall (London, 1954), pp. 54-74. This article is also found in G. Florovsky, *Bible, Church, Tradition: An Eastern Orthodox View,* Collected Works of G. Florovsky, 1 (Belmont, Mass., 1973). On this issue see also Vladimir Lossky, *In the Image and Likeness of God* (Crestwood, N.Y., 1974), especially the chapter entitled "Tradition and Traditions." Also, Thomas Hopko, *The Spirit of God* (Danbury, Conn., 1976).

25. *The Letters of St. Anthony the Great,* trans. Derwas J. Chitty (Oxford, 1977), pp. 10, 15, 22, 25 and 27.

26. See V. Lossky, *The Mystical Theology of the Eastern Church,* pp. 46-64; and *In the Image and Likeness of God,* pp. 13-139.

27. *The Vespers of Pentecost* (New York, 1974), p. 49.

28. St. Gregory of Nyssa, *On the Canticle of Canticles, PG* 44: 1049B-52A. See Daniélou and Musurillo, *From Glory to Glory,* pp. 273-74.

29. Romans 12.5; I Corinthians 10.17, 12.12-27; Galatians 6.15.

30. St. Cyril of Jerusalem, *Lectures on the Christian Sacraments* (Crestwood, N.Y., 1977), p. 61.

31. *Service Book* . . . , p. 281. See 2 Corinthians 1.22; Ephesians 1.13, 4.30. For a summary of patristic interpretations of the sacramental mysteries of the Church, see Jean Daniélou, *The Bible and the Liturgy* (Notre Dame, Ind., 1956). For a contemporary Orthodox interpretation, see Alexander Schmemann, *For the Life of the World* and *Of Water and the Spirit* (Crestwood, N.Y., 1963 and 1974).

32. Ephesians 1.10; Colossians 1.20. See also Nicholas Cabasilas (1322-1387) *The Life in Christ* and *A Commentary on the Divine Liturgy* (Crestwood, N.Y., 1974 and 1977).

33. Psalm 19.1, 50.6, 69.34 *et al.* Also, *The Song of the Three Youths.*

34. See Philippians 2.5-11.

35. The prayer at the Orthodox Divine Liturgy before the reception of Holy Communion says: "Not unto judgment, nor unto condemnation be my participation in Thy Holy Mysteries, O Lord, but for the healing of soul and body."

36. St. Symeon the New Theologian, *Practical and Theological Precepts* 48, 107 and 114, quoted from *Writings from the Philokalia on Prayer of the Heart,* trans. Kadloubovsky and Palmer (London, 1951), pp. 48, 122-24.

STARETZ SILOUAN:
A MODERN ORTHODOX SAINT
by
Theodore Stylianopoulos

"O what a Lord is ours!... If the Lord is ours, then all things are ours. That is how rich we are."[1] Echoing the language of St. Paul, Staretz[2] Silouan touches on the essence of Christian existence. For him Christian life is knowing Jesus Christ Who became poor so that we might become rich (cf. II Cor. 8:9). Silouan lived in awe and wonder at the glory of the Lord and His love for all creation. The centrality of God's love for the world and Christ's glorious victory over sin and death mark Silouan's life with the special qualities observed in Orthodox saints: Easter joy, encompassing love and spiritual radiance. The opportunity to examine the life and thought of Silouan is an invitation to explore some of the riches of sainthood in the Eastern Orthodox Church. Silouan exemplifies many central aspects of Orthodox spirituality in which he was deeply nurtured.

We are fortunate to know about Silouan through his disciple Archimandrite Sophrony. In 1948, ten years after Silouan's death, Sophrony wrote a volume in Russian about Silouan's life and writings which was subsequently published in Paris under the saint's name (1952). An English translation of this volume was published in 1958 entitled *The Undistorted Image*.[3] Recently a rivised and expanded edition of this work came out in two small volumes, one entitled *The Monk of Mount Athos*[4] and the other *Wisdom from Mount Athos*,[5] which are the main sources for the saint's life and thought. The first is an interpretive account of the life and teaching of Silouan. It offers personal reflections of someone who intimately knew him and provides insights especially into the spiritual struggles of the saint. The second book, edited also by Sophrony, contains the teachings of Silouan. These teachings were set down during the last years of the saint's life in the form of inspired notations.

The title of the second book, *Wisdom from Mount Athos,* in one respect does not correctly reflect the spiritual message of Silouan. Silouan's teachings are, to be sure, gems of spiritual wisdom but the saint would not think of them in this way. What he has to communicate to his readers is a gospel, a divine message: to know Jesus Christ through the power of the Holy Spirit. He writes with evangelical fervor and his words, even in translation, radiate apostolic power. Both of the above books, however, are valuable contributions to the spiritual witness of Silouan whose life reaches down to our own times. The present appreciation of Silouan and his teaching is based on these two books.

Born Simeon Ivanovich Antonov in the year 1866, Silouan lived the ordinary life of a Russian peasant. He was an honest, strong young man much impressed by the wisdom of his pious unlettered father. Simeon himself received little formal education. He went to school for only "two winters," as he said, probably just enough to learn how to read and write. His youth was marked by an inner yearning for God. This was highlighted by incidents in his early life.[6] Already at the age of nineteen he expressed the desire to enter the monastic life. However family considerations and sins of youth, with which the saint was not untouched, diminished the divine calling in him.

A particular incident served as a kind of turning point in his life. It was a jolting vision after a period of careless living. While Simeon on one occasion dozed off to sleep he dreamed that a snake crawled down his throat. He awakened full of horror and revulsion. He immediately heard a sweet voice saying: "Just as you found it loathsome to swallow a snake in your dream, so I find your ways ugly to look upon."[7] Simeon was convinced that the Virgin Mary herself spoke to him and was trying to lift him up from a life of corruption and spiritual death. This experience signaled in him a deep consciousness of sin and a profound need for repentance. These were foundations for his later spiritual heights. At the age of twenty-six, as soon as he finished his military service, Simeon entered the Russian monastery of St. Panteleimon on Mount Athos or, as it is called, the Holy Mountain. Mount Athos, an Aegean peninsula in northern Greece,

Staretz Silouan: A Modern Orthodox Saint

is the site of a cluster of more than twenty monastic communities and the greatest monastic center of the Orthodox Church.

The young novice set upon his monastic duties and the life of prayer with singular devotion. As in the case of each novice, Simeon was given a prayer rope (a "rosary") and was taught the Jesus Prayer—"Lord Jesus Christ, Son of God, have mercy on me, a sinner"—which he practiced with great zeal. The first spiritual fruits soon followed. He writes: "One day when I was a young novice I was praying before the icon of the Mother of God, and the Jesus Prayer entered into my heart."[8] This is a high state of spiritual prayer, known to Orthodox saints and fathers, in which the invocation of the Name of Jesus works spontaneously and uninterruptedly in the heart by the action of the Holy Spirit. Called the prayer of the heart, it is a high spiritual gift. Not long afterward Simeon was granted an even more sublime experience which he later intimated to his disciple Sophrony. According to the latter,[9] Simeon, while at Vespers, near the icon of the Savior, had a vision of the living Christ Himself. This was the decisive experience of his life. His whole being was filled with the grace of the Holy Spirit. He experienced a profound sense of forgiveness and reconciliation. Joy and peace flooded his soul. This was a new spiritual birth. Silouan himself is reticent about the actual vision. But he hints at this profound experience here and there in his own notes. On one occasion he writes:

> In the first year of my life in the monastery my soul apprehended God in the Holy Spirit... I turned to God for forgiveness, and He granted to me not forgiveness alone but the Holy Spirit, and I knew God in the Holy Spirit.[10]

And again: "It was given to me, a poor sinner, through the Holy Spirit to know that Jesus Christ is God."[11] And elsewhere he testifies:

> I brought nothing but sins with me to the monastery, and I do not know why, when I was still a young novice, the Lord gave me the grace of the Holy Spirit... I did not ask the Lord for the Holy Spirit: I did not know about the Holy Spirit and how He enters the soul, nor what He does with the soul; but now it

is a great joy for me to write of this. O Holy Spirit, how dear art Thou to the soul!¹²

Three years later, at the age of thirty, Simeon was professed a monk, receiving the name of Silouan in accordance with the monastic tradition of changing name as a sign of a radical change in life. For most of his forty-six years as a monk, Silouan worked in the monastery flour mill and was also one of the monastery stewards serving in the kitchen and dining room. He never became externally significant. He quietly carried out his duties without attracting attention to himself. His disciple Sophrony cites several humorous incidents about important persons later coming to seek the spiritual advice of the Staretz to the surprise of some of his fellow monks who did not have eyes to see what a treasure they had in Silouan.

In one such incident a prominent and learned monk, Father Stratonicos, came to visit Mount Athos from the Russian Caucasus. He was well-known for his spiritual gifts. But he came to the Holy Mountain to find someone with whom he could profitably discuss several matters of concern to him. After two months of visiting various monasteries he began to feel that his long and arduous journey had perhaps been in vain for he had not learned anything new. Then he incidentally discovered Silouan. They talked privately on several occasions. Afterwards Father Statonicos became quiet and deeply thoughtful. Another monk asked him: "What is wrong with you, Father Stratonicos? I don't recognize you . . . You sit there mournfully, your inspired lips sealed. What is the matter?" "How should I answer your questions?" replied Stratonicos. "It is not good for me to speak. You have Silouan. Ask him." The monk who had asked the questions looked amazed. He had known Silouan for a long time and respected him . But he never thought of asking him for any advice.¹³

Silouan grew in the spiritual life but not without severe struggles. An initial period of spiritual exaltation followed his vision of Christ and his new birth by the Spirit. But this experience began to diminish in him. Severe struggles followed. The questions that now emerged with great significance to him were:

How can one remain alive to the gentle grace of the Holy Spirit? Once illumined, why does the mind become dark and dull again? How can one grow to spiritual stability? Silouan himself makes reference to his spiritual struggles. He writes, hinting at the causes of his soul's turmoil:

> Twice was I beguiled. The first time was at the beginning when I was a young novice, and came about because of my inexperience; and the Lord was swift to forgive me. But the second occasion was due to pride, and that time I suffered a long torment before the Lord healed me.[14]

It was through such struggles that Silouan learned more deeply about spiritual vigilance, the subtle warfare with pride, the cleansing of the heart and complete reliance on God. It may be here noted that Silouan's spiritual life was moulded through the traditional Orthodox monastic disciplines such as liturgy, the life of prayer, reading of the Bible and the reading of the Church Fathers. Although Silouan had little formal education, he became during his years as a monk, well-schooled in the liturgical texts, Holy Scripture and the spiritual writings of Church Fathers. These were the sources, along with prayer, that provided the nourishment for Silouan's spiritual growth and knowledge of God.

Silouan's most precious lesson was about humility. Humility seemed like a key which unlocked a deeper knowledge of the mysteries of God's Kingdom. Having discerned and renounced spiritual pride, Silouan was especially drawn to the humility of Christ. He received a richer illumination of grace which enabled him intuitively to understand the truths of Scripture and the spiritual teachings of the Church Fathers. Grace no longer seemed to leave him as before. Temptations diminished. Greater spiritual stability prevailed. His soul increased in joy and gratitude for all things. A deep love flowed from his heart for all people and for all creatures and wonders of creation.

One of the most distinctive aspects of Silouan's life was his personal witness or testimony, reminiscent of St. Symeon the New Theologian (949-1022 AD), another Spirit-filled Orthodox saint. Silouan was a man of God. He had come to know God deeply and personally. The fire of divine love consumed him. Externally he was a quiet, simple, and gentle man who carried countless sacks of flour around the mill of St. Panteleimon's monastery. He lacked the aggressiveness of St. Symeon the New Theologian. He sought to instruct no one. He writes: "All my desire is to learn humility and the love of Christ that I may offend no man and pray for all as I pray for myself."[15] But inwardly his soul was a dwelling-place of the Holy Spirit. As in the case of the Prophet Jeremiah and of St. Paul, the consuming fire that burned his inward parts did not permit him to remain silent but rather led him toward the end of his life to write about God's love for the world. He exclaims:

> My soul loves the Lord, and how may I hide this fire which warms my soul? How shall I hide the Lord's mercies in which my soul delights? How can I hold my peace, with my soul captive to God? How shall I be silent when my spirit is consumed day and night with love for Him?[16]

Silouan did not stir those immediately around him nor create any controversies. But his written word carries authority as a personal witness on behalf of God, such as in the case of the Prophets, Apostles and Evangelists. He states: "I write out of the grace of God. Yea, this is truth. The Lord Himself is my witness."[17]

Silouan did not write in order to write. He did not himself simply decide to write. Like many spiritual writers before him, he wrote because of the inner prompting of the Holy Spirit. He wrote at the end of his life, after his long spiritual struggles, when he had deeply matured in grace and was beyond the subtle influence of pride. He does not write about himself, although he seems to make the daring claim of having within him the same grace which empowered the Prophets and Apostles. He writes about the Lord. He thinks of himself as insignificant. His personal concerns completely recede behind the reality of the glory of God and the need to call all men to repentance. Can a single soul be saved? That was the crucial question. He says: "My soul knows His mercy towards me, and I write of it in hope that even one soul may come to love the Lord and be turned to Him by the fire of repentance."[18]

Silouan addressed himself not only to his contemporaries but to all. The love of God, the call to repentance, the need for forgiveness and the experience of reconciliation in the Holy Spirit are permanent issues relevant to every generation. There is in Silouan a profound note of catholic truth and a genuine universal concern which flow from his soul. Silouan's heart burned with love not only for Orthodox Christians, not for Christians alone, but for all human beings. For him all persons on every corner of the earth were part of the people of God. Silouan's soul calls out to all. Here are some typical statements from his notations:

> I cannot remain silent concerning the people, whom I love so greatly that I must weep for them.[19]
>
> My heart aches for the whole world, and I pray and shed tears for the whole world, that all may repent and know God, and live in love, and delight in freedom in God. . . . O all ye peoples of the earth, pray and weep for your sins, that the Lord may forgive them.[20]
>
> O ye peoples of the earth, fashioned by God, know your Creator and His love for us. . . .
> Turn to Him, all ye peoples of the earth. . . .
> Know all ye peoples that we are created for the glory of God. . . .Cleave not to the earth, for God is our Father and He loves us like beloved children.[21]

Silouan is a man with a message. He is an evangelist. He writes with a spiritual directness reminiscent of St. John and St. Paul. He is totally involved in a deeply personal way both with God and with man. Not infrequently, like St. Paul, the ambassador of Christ who beseeched persons to be reconciled to God (II Cor. 5:20), Silouan pleads with people on behalf of God, as one pleads with dearly beloved brothers. His was an inner loving authority received directly from God. His notations have the character of a prophetic witness. He does not write with intellectual arguments to convince the mind. He writes as a man of God to convert the heart. Let us now turn to some major topics which concerned him such as knowledge of God, the Holy Spirit, prayer, the inner spiritual struggle, and the criteria of authentic spiritual life.

1. Knowledge of God

Silouan's life was centered on knowing God. Through his spiritual journey he had come to see with absolute clarity that what finally matters in life is just this: who comes to know God and who does not. He taught that the most precious thing in the world is to know God and to understand His will, even if only in part. Nothing is more precious than to know God; nothing is more disastrous than not to know Him. Here are echoes of the great teaching of theocentricity which radiates from the life and thought of all men of deep faith.

For Silouan, knowledge of God was direct and immediate— personal communion with Him. One may know about God and still not know Him personally. The Lord became incarnate and a multitude of people beheld Him in the flesh, but not all knew Him as Lord. So it is now. Many may know about Christ but do not know Him by personal experience. Silouan distinguished between believing in Christ and knowing Christ. However, he did not criticize the implicit faith of Christians. To believe in Christ is also a blessed thing, he taught, according to the words of the Lord to Thomas: "Blessed are those who have not seen and yet believe" (Jn 20:29). Yet there is another "seeing," not merely a "believing," open to every Christian. Such knowledge of Christ is not a human achievement but a gift of the Holy Spirit. When the soul which yearns for the Lord finds Him through the Holy Spirit, and knows Him, from that hour its love for the Lord is greater than any other love.

Silouan draws a similar distinction between learning about God through studies, books and research, and knowing Him through the Holy Spirit. Many philosophers and scholars may have arrived at a belief in God, but they have not come to know God. There is a great difference between affirming that God exists or observing His works in nature or even seeing His truths in Scripture, and, on the other hand, knowing God through personal communion with Him. No earthly science can adequately teach us about God. Staretz Silouan knew educated men and respected them. He never talked against education. He was not an obscurantist. However, he was convinced that God is not made known through ordinary learning. There are those who spend their whole lives seeking knowledge of the world and the things in it; yet this is of no profit to the soul. A person can even earn a doctorate in theology and know what others have said and have thought about God, yet not know God Himself. Sometimes knowledge through books and learning can become an obstacle to knowing God, not because reason and human wisdom are negative in themselves, but because they can lead to pride, intellectual arrogance, and a false sense of self-sufficiency.

How is the Lord to be known? Silouan does not develop a theoretical answer to this question but simply points to the daily Christian life, to prayer and to deep yearning for the Lord. He especially emphasizes that unless the Lord grants us knowledge of Himself we cannot know Him as we should. Revelation is personal. Only God reveals God. We may study as much as we will and think as much as we will, but we cannot control or compel God through human skill, ingenuity or wisdom. The Lord makes Himself known to repentant hearts through the Holy Spirit. The Holy Spirit, sweet and gracious, draws the soul to love the Lord. Writes Silouan:

> If you would know of the Lord's love for us, hate sin and wrong thoughts, and day and night pray fervently. The Lord will then give you His grace and you will known Him through the Holy Spirit, and after death, when you enter into paradise, there too you will know the Lord through the Holy Spirit, as you knew Him on earth.[22]

Knowledge of God is not a matter of speculation but of experience:

> We are able to treat of God only in so far as we have known the grace of the Holy Spirit; for how can a man think on and consider a thing that he has not seen or heard tell of, and does not know? Now the saints declare that they have seen God; yet there are people who say that God is not. No doubt they say this inasmuch as they have not known God, but it does not

at all mean that He is not. The saints speak of that which they have actually seen, of that which they know.[23]

According to Silouan, each Christian should seek personal knowledge of God as his primary life-goal. A Christian does not need special learning nor special methods. He needs only to love his neighbor, be humble, obedient and fervent in prayer. How personal knowledge of God occurs cannot be explained but that it does occur is an absolute certainty. The soul suddenly sees the Lord and knows that it is He. Love and peace flood the soul. "Who shall describe this joy, this gladness?" asks Silouan. The soul experiences the Lord as a dear guest and seeks after Him with great yearning. Abiding in His presence and having daily fellowship with the divine Guest transform life into a spiritual feast in which the believer rejoices every day and every hour.

2. The Holy Spirit

Because the Staretz constantly talks about the Holy Spirit in the most personal and tender fashion, it is worth pointing out several of his teachings on the Holy Spirit. According to the saint, the Lord schools us through His Word and His Holy Spirit. He makes us kin with Him. The Holy Spirit dwells in us and transforms us into the likeness of Christ. By the Holy Spirit Christ unites us with God and makes us one family with the Father. Without the Holy Spirit the soul has no life. The person who has the Holy Spirit feels that he has paradise within himself.

The Holy Spirit is love and sweetness to the whole person. He pervades a person's entire being—soul, mind and body. A man who comes to know the Lord by the Holy Spirit stands in awe and wonder before the Lord. The Holy Spirit is like a dear mother. He lovingly cares for us, forgives and heals us, illumines and rejoices us. However, counsels Silouan, we must guard the grace of the Holy Spirit with prayerful vigilance—a single evil thought and He forsakes the soul. Unless we repent, the love of God remains no longer with us.

According to Silouan, the Holy Spirit is the power which unites the Church Triumphant and the Church Militant. The communion of glorified saints, the hosts of angels and the faithful on earth are all bound together by the grace of the Holy Spirit. The same Holy Spirit is in heaven and on earth and unites the whole wondrous assembly of God: the Virgin Mary, the angels, the saints, the Patriarchs, the Prophets, the Apostles, the Martyrs and all believers. We on earth are bound to the communion of saints through the Holy Spirit. Our spirits burn with love for them and their spirits burn with love for us. If love enables one not to forget a brother, how much more do the saints remember and pray for us. It is by the power of the Holy Spirit that we can know and pray to the saints. When we pray to them, they hear our prayers in the Holy Spirit. Silouan exhorts Christians to pray to the Virgin Mary and to the saints. It was his conviction that they hear our prayers and even know our innermost thoughts. Intimates Silouan: "Marvel not at this. Heaven and all the saints live by the Holy Spirit, and in all the world there is nothing hidden from the Holy Spirit... they see us in the Holy Spirit and know our entire lives."[24]

3. Prayer

Prayer occupies the central position in the spirituality of the Orthodox Church. Progress in spiritual life is almost identified with progress in prayer. By prayer is meant not only frequent private and corporate prayer, but a life of prayer—a spiritual condition of the heart by which the believer prayerfully lives, thinks and acts with spontaneous awareness of the presence of God. Because of the personal nature of prayer and the immediacy with which it brings the believer before the living God, prayer is the delicate instrument which, by its depth and warmth, measures a person's spiritual growth. Silouan's life was dominated by prayer. From the day he entered the monastery he practiced the Jesus Prayer and soon was granted true prayer of the heart through the grace of the Holy Spirit. It is no wonder that Silouan found prayer a mighty weapon in his struggles and a key to the spiritual life.

Silouan has some simple but profound thoughts to share with his readers on prayer. Prayer is equally for all. The best thing one can do is simply to pray with whatever strength and knowledge he may have. God will honor the longing and the efforts of one who struggles in prayer and will give him more strength and knowledge in prayer. A child cannot walk except by taking his first steps. Prayer comes with praying. But it must be contrite and sincere. Instructs Silouan: "The Lord will give prayer to him who prays; and he of experience will know the assurance and love for God that comes to the mind. Although he be a sinful man·the Lord will grant him to taste the fruits of prayer."[25]

Silouan nowhere gives a formal definition of prayer. Yet it is clear from his notations that true spiritual prayer is to dwell with the mind and heart unceasingly with God. To think of God is already a prayer. The Staretz counsels that he who makes it a habit to think of God always carries God in his soul, just as one who always thinks of worldly things is absorbed by them. The more a believer thinks of God, the more he is fired with love and fervor towards Him. He who loves the Lord is always mindful of Him and remembrance of God begets prayer. But without prayer who can love God? If one is forgetful of God, he will not dwell in the love of God, for the grace of the Holy Spirit which fires the soul with divine love comes through prayer.

Prayer is always and everywhere possible. The soul is the true temple of God. For the man who prays in his heart the whole universe is a church, says Silouan. Unceasing thanksgivings, spiritual songs and praises can go on in the believer's heart whose life is thus transformed into a living sacrifice to God. This is the true spiritual worship of which Christ spoke. No form of activity necessarily interferes with the person who yearns to abide in Christ and to practice daily inward prayer. The person who loves God can keep Him in mind day and night. But, warns Silouan, fault-finding, idle talk and self-indulgence are the death of prayer.

What is one to ask in prayer? The believer should pray for understanding in all things and about what to do in all situations. Genuine prayer is accompanied by peace of God in the soul and by a tender feeling towards every living thing. For the believer who prays in a humble manner, the Lord Himself is the teacher.

The Lord, Who mercifully watches over us, will not lead us astray. Silouan was aware of people's doubts about the efficacy of prayer and fears about deception. For Silouan the fruits of prayer, such as divine love, humility, compassion, peace and joy, testify to the veracity of prayer. Here is what he writes:

> Some there are who say that prayer beguiles. This is not so. A man is beguiled by listening to his own self, and not by prayer. All the saints lived in prayer, and called others to prayer. Prayer is the path to God. By prayer we obtain humility, patience and every good gift. The man who speaks against prayer has manifestly never experienced the goodness of the Lord, and how greatly He loves us. No evil ever comes from God. All the saints prayed without ceasing: they filled every moment with prayer.[26]

What about the problem of unanswered prayer? According to Silouan not one prayer nor a single good thought is lost with God. However, God sometimes seems remote to us. We pray but God seems not to hear us. There may be several reasons for this, says the saint. First, what we ask may be improper. Secondly, it may not be to our spiritual benefit. Finally, pride may separate us from nearness to God and invalidate our prayers.

The highest form of prayer is the interior prayer of the heart, a spontaneous invocation of the Name of Jesus Christ. This uninterrupted calling upon the Name of the Lord, which is a gift, must be sought with great care, love and humility. God bestows His gifts on the humble. When a person is mindful of the Lord, obedient and humble in all things, he receives the gift of interior prayer from the Lord Himself, and such prayer continues without difficulty deep in the heart. When one attains to such perfect prayer and continually dwells in God, he acquires such spiritual sensitivity that in all his conversations with others and in all his dealings with things he does not speak and act, as it were, from "his own mind" but he speaks and acts according to the promptings of the Holy Spirit. Such a person has become the dwelling place of the Holy Spirit and has acquired the mind of Christ. This dynamic state of prayer is a sublime gift and, cautions Silouan, one should not be presumptuous to think for himself that he has attained it. It is best to keep one's mind on Christ and avoid self-conscious attention either to the fruits or heights of prayer.

4. The Spiritual Struggle

In the tradition of Orthodox spirituality one meets recurrent themes about repentance, decision, firm resolve, vigilance, obedience and inner spiritual warfare. These themes are not new but derive from the Bible. Jesus and John the Baptist radically called their hearers to repentance. St. Paul frequently exhorts Christians to be sober, vigilant and to put on the whole armor of God—always ready to wage spiritual battle. Jesus also said that keen and daring persons take hold of God's Kingdom.

For all the Apostles and saints grace is a gift; it is something to be received rather than to be earned. Salvation is primarily the work of God, not of man. Nevertheless each Christian participates in the mystery of salvation through a personal response of his total being, beginning with a fundamental decision to turn from oneself and the world to God as the center and source of life. This is nothing less than a conversion to God and taking up battle against sin and evil. The Lord battled unceasingly with evil and lived in comlete obedience to His Father. So also each Christian is called to wage ceaseless spiritual warfare against evil and sin in complete obedience to God. Man does not save himself. God alone saves. But to receive God's blessings and gifts the Christian must respond to God with all of his inner and outer resources. God both demands and deserves a Christian's best in total surrender to Him.

Staretz Silouan was an accomplished warrior of Christ. He knew that spiritual warfare is at once simple and complex, easy and difficult. It is complex and difficult because of the cunning of the human heart. A human being does not easily abandon self-love nor quickly surrender the ego to God. It is simple and easy because of the grace of God. Writes Silouan:

> Fierce is the war we wage; yet it is a wise and simple one. If the soul grows to love humility, then all the snares of our ene-

mies are overturned and his fortresses taken.... The war is a stubborn war, but only for the proud: the humble find it easy because they love the Lord and He gives them the powerful armament of the grace of the Holy Spirit.[27]

The spiritual struggle begins with *metanoia* (repentance). Repentance is a thorough conversion of the mind and heart to God. It is a profound yes to God which leads to the establishment of new attitudes, new priorities and new values. A person cannot even begin spiritual warfare without this fundamental turning to God to receive His help. Without the Holy Spirit, declares Silouan, the soul is incapable even of starting out upon the race. The soul neither knows nor understands who and where her enemies are. Without God's unfailing guidance, the soul stumbles and falls at every turn. Therefore, the whole basis of spiritual warfare is to place God at the center of life. Victory depends on complete reliance on God. But surrender and obedience to God do not at all imply passivity. What is surrendered is not action but self-will, not creative thought but selfish drives. The Christian can be highly active—in fact divine grace releases his inner gifts in a most effective manner—but a Christian's activity is always God-centered and love-centered. According to Orthodox saints, "passivity" is a state of being controlled by inner moods, drives and passions which the inner self obeys like a slave, whether or not a person is externally "active." True "activity" is prayer, a dynamic spiritual condition of being in conscious communion with God and freely choosing the good through cooperation with divine grace.

Because of pride which leads man to self-reliance, it is usually by affliction that man recognizes his insufficiency and turns to God. The Lord dearly loves man, teaches Silouan, but He allows affliction so that man may perceive his weakness, his need of God, and entrust himself to his Creator. When a Christian exalts himself or subtly lapses into self-reliance, God withdraws from him and delivers him to suffering. Suffering is not only outward, such as some illness or physical hardship, which are unavoidable in life. But suffering is above all inward—the lacerations of the soul. Without God, the soul experiences distress, fear and conflict, or dejection, emptiness and unfulfillment. It often finds itself in darkness, tormented by fantasies, frustration and evil thoughts. Silouan notes that the soul continues to suffer until it humbles itself and turns to the Lord in repentance. It is a short step to the light of God. After repentance, the simplest path to spiritual life is described as follows by Silouan:

> Be obedient and sober, do not find fault, and keep mind and heart from evil thoughts (through prayer). Remember that all men are good and beloved of the Lord. For such humility the grace of the Holy Spirit will dwell in you, and cause you to exclaim, "How merciful is the Lord!" But if you find fault and are rebellious, if you want your own way, your soul will fail and you will cry: "The Lord has forgotten me!" But it is not the Lord Who has forgotten you: it is you who have forgotten that you must humble yourself, and so the grace of God abides not in your soul.[28]

Spiritual warfare is primarily a matter of the mind and heart. Jesus said that all thoughts proceed from the heart—the inner man. The crucial battleground is mostly unseen. The Orthodox saints called the spiritual struggle ἀόρατος πόλεμος (invisible warfare). What is at stake is control of the inner thought world by grace or by other forces. St. Paul spoke of having the mind of Christ. This exactly is the goal of spiritual life: to acquire the mind of Christ. The inner man can allow grace to control and transfigure all thinking, decisions and commitments. On the negative side, the inner person must alertly reject all evil thoughts and in no way obey sinful promptings. Silouan counsels his readers to cut off sin at the root by rejecting evil thoughts immediately through prayer. Should an evil thought arise in the mind, or an evil inclination disturb the heart, let the Christian quickly turn to Christ through inner prayer. The Jesus Prayer, brief and powerful, is most effective in invisible warfare. If one becomes forgetful, fails to chase away evil thoughts, and assents to them, he must at once repent to God. Otherwise the force of evil will grow in him and soon will express itself through actions and then habits. It is easier to uproot a blade of grass than a tree, another Orthodox saint once remarked. Not only evil thoughts, but also daydreaming, empty fantasies, and irrelevant thoughts often intrude, preoccupy the mind, confuse it, and subtly deceive it into evil. The outcome is the mind's separation from God which brings spiritual darkness. Another Orthodox saint called the mind "a wagon-full of monkeys." There can be no inner relief from them—no freedom from inner disturbance and confusion—without frequent prayer and vigilant resolve to follow the guidance of the Holy Spirit. According to Silouan, a Christian cannot fulfill the Lord's commandment to love God with all of his mind, heart and soul until useless thoughts are replaced by heavenly ones and the Christian is inwardly transformed through the renewal of his mind.

So the battle rages on and will not cease until death. Condemn your brother and you lose peace. Be boastful and grace leaves you. Tarry with evil thoughts and you lose confidence in prayer. Be fond of glory, power or material gains and you lose experience of God's love. Follow your own will and you are conquered by the enemy. Hate your brother, judge him, and you fall away from God into the control of an evil spirit. "Be sober, be watchful. Your adversary the devil prowls around like a roaring lion, seeking some one to devour" (1 Pt. 5:8).

Staretz Silouan exhorts: Let not an hour pass without repentance. Do not lose the peace of the Holy Spirit over trifles. Surrender to the Lord so that He may guide you with His mighty hand. Guard the grace of God; without it man is but sinful clay. As a man nourishes himself with food, so also he should sustain himself through the grace of the Holy Spirit. Without the Holy Spirit the soul is spiritually dead. Love your enemies, pray for those who insult or injure you, and offer thanks to God for all things. This is the narrow and hard way of the Christian struggle to spiritual victory by God's grace.

5. Two Criteria of Authentic Spirituality

"Test the spirits," admonishes St. John (I Jn 4:1). What are the chief signs of genuine spiritual life? Staretz Silouan knew well the subtleties of the spiritual struggle and how easily man falls prey to pride and vainglory. He especially emphasized two criteria of authentic Christian life: love and humility. In his own struggles Silouan was drawn more and more to Christ's humble, self-emptying love for all people and for all creation. Silouan lived the strict life of Athonite monasticism but his spirit was not rigid, doctrinaire, self-righteous or triumphalistic. He strove to understand and to serve every person. Those who differed with him he treated with gentleness and respect. He was a man with a child-like, tender heart. Spontaneous love radiated from him and embraced all without differentiation.

Silouan held a remarkably enlightened view of people of other faiths. He would not pronounce judgment on any person, far or near. Sure of his own faith experience, he intuitively sensed that God has His ways with all of the world's people whom He loves dearly. Silouan constantly prayed that all people might turn to God and come to know His love. Once in a conversation with a certain hermit, the latter declared with evident satisfaction: "God will punish all atheists. They will burn in everlasting fire." Distressed with such an attitude, Father Silouan replied: "Tell me, supposing you went to paradise and there looked down and saw somebody in hell-fire—would you feel happy?" The hermit responded: "It can't be helped. It would be their own fault." Silouan said: "Love could not bear that. We must pray for all."[29]

Silouan shed many tears especially for those who did not know God. He wrote: "Day and night I pray to the Lord for love, and the Lord gives me tears to weep for the whole world."[30] This is an image of how God loves us, gently and without reproach, just as the father of the Gospel story did not reproach his prodigal son. When a Christian experiences such love everything rejoices in him. When he loses awareness of it, he can not find peace, is troubled, blames others and does not realize that he himself is at fault. Love of God and love of neighbor are the highest aspects of the Christian experience. Without them life becomes burdensome. Silouan is lyrical about God's love:

> O brethren, there is nothing better than the love of God when the Lord fires the soul with love for God and our fellow-man.

The man who knows the delight of the love of God...loves both God and man (and) knows in part that the Kingdom of God is within us. Blessed is the soul that loves her brother, for our brother is our life.[31]

Divine love, according to Silouan, reaches out to all things, creatures and plants. A story in the newspapers some time ago related how a dog jumped into a well after a three year old boy and held him up until the lad was rescued. Love is in all things and unites all things. A person must respond with love not only to people but also to nature and everything in it. Here are Silouan's words about a simple leaf and man:

> That green leaf on the tree which you needlessly plucked: it was not wrong, only rather a pity for the little leaf. The heart that has learned to love feels sorry for every created thing. But man is a supreme creation, and therefore if you see that he has gone astray and is bringing destruction upon himself pray for him... the soul that acts after this fashion is loved of the Lord, for she is like unto Him.[32]

The highest expression of love, and the surest criterion of Christian truth, is love of enemies. True love cannot suffer a single soul to perish. For Christ there are no "enemies," for the very word implies rejection. They are brothers who need our love and prayers. Christ prayed for those who crucified Him. St. Stephen prayed for those who stoned him. So we must urge ourselves to love those who revile or injure us. If we cannot love, at least let us not revile. A person who reviles or despises those who are against him, brings spiritual injury to himself and shows that an evil spirit is working in him. But divine love cannot be attained by man without divine grace. We cannot love our enemies without having the Holy Spirit. When we humble ourselves and pray for those who affront us, God works impossible things in the heart. On one occasion Silouan states that the soul is so wounded by divine love that it loses its wits. Even devils can rouse its pity because they were once God's creatures now fallen from the good.

The second criterion of authentic spiritual life is humility. "Were I to be asked," declares Staretz Silouan, "what would I have of God, what gifts, I should answer: 'The spirit of humility in which the Lord rejoices above all things.'"[33] Silouan learned true humility after years of intense struggles which seemed to cast him into the abyss of despair. According to the Staretz, one night while yet in the midst of his struggles, his cell was filled with devils. One large devil stood in front of him so that Silouan could not pray before his icon without seemingly worshiping the foul creature. Silouan prayed fervently to God saying: "Tell me what I must do that they may leave me." The Lord's reply was: "The proud always suffer from many devils. . . . Keep your mind in hell, and despair not."[34] According to Silouan's interpretation, this was not a counsel of despair but an admonition to check spiritual pride. Let the Christian keep his mind on his sinfulness and the judgment of hell, but let him despair not because of God's love which forgives, reconciles and saves.

True humility is the crucifixion of self-will and obedience to God's will under all circumstances and in all things. The whole spiritual warfare wages around humility because the proud man does not want to obey God. He likes to be his own master. But where there is pride there cannot be grace. Fight the evil one, exhorts Silouan, with the weapon of humility. Humility is the principal power. The soul of the humble man is like the sea: throw a stone into the sea—for a moment it will ruffle the surface of the water a little, and then sink to the bottom. We are not humble and therefore we torment ourselves and others. We boast and compete over trifles, and so make ourselves and others unhappy. The humble soul enjoys great peace, while the proud soul is a torment to itself.

The Christian can lapse into self-assurance and spiritual pride in subtle ways. Here is what Staretz Silouan writes from his own experience:

> At first when a man begins to work for the Lord grace gives him the strength to be zealous after good, all is easy and effortless; and seeing this, in his inexperience he thinks to himself: 'I shall continue thus zealously all my life long,' and at the same time he exalts himself above those who live carelessly, and begins to pass judgment on them (inwardly or outwardly). And so he loses the grace that was helping him to keep God's commandments. And he does not understand what happened—

everything was going so well with him, but now it is all so difficult and he feels no desire to pray.[35]

If such a person who exalts himself over his fellows does not humble himself and repent, a ravaging inner struggle begins. He becomes inwardly oppressed until he turns to the Lord. But suffering will profit him nothing if he does not humble himself. So long as the soul lacks humility, wrong thoughts and evil impulses will always torment it. But when the soul humbles itself, it will find forgiveness, serenity and holiness in God.

Silouan was greatly attracted to the humility of Christ Who said: "Learn from me; for I am gentle and lowly in heart" (Mt. 11:29). The Staretz instructs Christians to take great pains to preserve the humble spirit of Christ, for without it the light of grace is extinguished and the soul dies. Some, says Silouan, after many years of struggle, do not understand why things are not well with them, why they do not feel peace and their souls are cast down. The reason is that they have not walked the humble way of the Lord but inwardly exalt themselves. But when the soul truly sees that the Lord is meek and lowly, it utterly humbles itself. Then the peace of Christ enters the soul and the soul, like Job, is glad to sit among the ashes and behold others in glory. From love the soul wishes every human being more good than it wishes itself, and delights when it sees others happier, and grieves when it sees them suffering. This is the way of the Lord.

NOTES

1. Archimandrite Sophrony, *Wisdom from Mount Athos,* trans. Rosemary Edmonds (New York, 1975), pp. 26-27.

2. "Staretz" in the Russian language is an elder who is a spiritual guide.

3. Trans. Rosemary Edmonds (London, 1958).

4. Trans. Rosemary Edmonds (Oxford, 1973).

5. See note 1.
6. *Monk,* pp. 7-9.
7. P. 11.
8. *Wisdom,* p. 59.
9. *Monk,* p. 19.
10. *Wisdom,* p. 37.
11. P. 19.
12. P. 104.
13. *Monk,* pp. 39-41.
14. *Wisdom,* p. 117.
15. P. 86.
16. Archimandrite Soprony, *His Life is Mine,* trans. Rosemary Edmonds (Oxford, 1977), p. 76.
17. *Wisdom,* p. 19.
18. P. 42.
19. P. 30.
20. Pp. 75-76.
21. P. 23.
22. P. 21.
23. P. 22.
24. P. 59.
25. P. 102.
26. P. 85.
27. P. 111.
28. Ibid.
29. *Monk,* p. 32.
30. *Wisdom,* p. 26.
31. P. 30.
32. P. 32.
33. P. 120.
34. Pp. 118-19.
35. Pp. 91-92.

THE DESERT FATHERS AS MODELS
FOR THE MONKS OF THE WEST
by
Joseph F. Kelly

In the first few centuries of Christian history, the Greek East frequently played the tutor to the Latin West. Much of what the West received from the East is well-known—a New Testament written in Greek, the great ecumenical councils, monasticism *inter alia*. This paper will consider a lesser known but no less fascinating aspect of the East to West flow, the influence on the religious life of the West of the Desert Fathers, those devout Eastern Christians, mostly Egyptians, who fled civilized society to find salvation in the solitude of the desert.[1]

All history depends upon historiography. The modern age can only work with what the past has given it. The writers who provided the accounts which this paper will use were not writing history, but rather hagiography, that is, the life of a saint, a work intended to be not just biographical but also—and primarily—didactic. The reader or listener of this life would not only learn about the saint but would also be impressed at the power of God at work in the saint and would desire to imitate so holy a person.[2]

Such an approach may sound too idealized for the twentieth century, but the early Christians expected, even demanded, that saints' lives be normative guides for Christian behavior. Indeed, many contemporary Christians unconsciously echo that approach because when they speak of the smooth, clean lines of the Early Church, they are more likely thinking of the praying, sharing, unified Christians of Acts of the Apostles 2:42-46 than of the incestuous, bibulous, fractious Christians of I Corinthians. The importance of hagiography will be evident throughout this paper.

How, why and when the retreat to the desert began is unknown. Scholars have contended that this movement was a natural outgrowth of Christian attitudes toward the world, sex, property *et cetera*. Others have contended that it derived from pagan practices such as philosophical detachment, Jewish practices such as the Essene withdrawal to the Dead Sea monasteries, or even Buddhist monasticism, an unlikely but historically possible occurrence given the contacts of Alexandria with Asia. Recently an American scholar, Richard E. Sullivan, has argued that monasticism was one of those rare historical phenomena, something new.[3]

The name of the first monk is unknown. The first known monk was the great Egyptian, Antony (ca. 251-356), but his hagiographer, Athanasios, bishop of Alexandria, says that he (Antony) followed the advice of an older solitary, so he could not have been the first.[4] The Latin writer Jerome, claiming to use information from Egyptian contacts, wrote a life of a certain Paul of Thebes as the first monk, but critics ancient and modern have thought Paul owes his existence to Jerome's pen and nothing more.[5] For all historical purposes, Athanasios' life of Antony provides the earliest account of desert monasticism, and the life of Antony—actual and literary—set the pattern for many other lives.

The first monks withdrew from the society of people to find salvation in personal, one-to-one encounters with God. They initially occupied chance accommodations, such as caves or the deserted fort Antony used, but later built for themselves little huts or cells. Occasionally some of these hermits would meet, either accidentally or by design, for spiritual advice and encouragement, but for the most part they preferred living alone.

Early in the fourth century, another great Egyptian monk, Pachomios (ca. 290-346) recognized that for many monks, the spirit was willing, but eremitic monasticism, that is, living as hermits, was too much. Consequently he instituted cenobitic monasticism, that is, monks living in a group. This form of monasticism grew increasingly popular until the hermits were reduced to a small proportion of the total monastic population, although the eremitic life-style remained something of an ideal. Both cenobites and eremites practiced rigid asceticism, that is, constant physical self-denial and even deliberate mor-

The Desert Fathers as Models for the Monks of the West 57

tification in order to control the body.

The home of the ascetics, the desert, played a Janus-like role in the hagiography. As an escape from civilization and its ills, the desert represented the return to the natural world, a sort of parched Garden of Paradise. But as the deserted place, a place without government or laws, it represented chaos, the home of the forces of disorder. In the desert the monks found God, but they also found the devil.

The devil plays a major role in the life of Antony and in the lives of most of the other ascetics. It has truly been said, "where there is a hermit, there is a devil."[6]

The accounts of the saints and the demons make marvelous popular reading—dramatic, suspenseful, occasionally disheartening, often encouraging. The ascetic travels alone in the desert. The fiend sees a potential victim and tries to frighten and intimidate the monk. The man of God holds fast, and the devil withdraws. Soon he returns in a more powerful attack, often with a troop of other fiends, and the poor hermit is buffeted about in this pandemonium. But again his faith saves him. Now the devil realizes that a frontal asault is useless; corruption will achieve more than coercion. So he looks for weaknesses. Visions of fine food and drink challenge his fasting. Visions of beautiful women challenge his continence. And if the hermit can withstand all of this, the devil plays his trump card: is not the holy man unjustly proud of his achievements and thus sinful after all? Some monks succumb to this; the true saints of God, of course, do not.

The accounts of the struggles with demons provide the literary mode for explaining a real situation—the terrible demands of the desert life which only the strongest and most stable could survive. One can only wonder how many monks overestimated their abilities and were driven out of their wits by the loneliness and desolation of the desert, or, for that matter, how many simply failed physically, dying of sheer exhaustion. But the accounts record few failures and many successes, and the successes, that is, the lives of the saints, have provided the traditional picture of monastic life.

The positive side of monastic life was the monks' firm conviction that their way of life was the best for them, was especially favored by God, and led to salvation. This attitude or perception also took on a specific literary form.

The ideal Christian life is the *imitatio Christi,* the imitation of Christ. All Christians should have the selfless, loving life of Jesus as their goal, and if the life of Jesus seems too remote by virtue of its perfection, the lives of other biblical figures were within reach. Monastic hagiography routinely portrayed its subjects as imitating Christ or other biblical figures. To an extent, this makes the hagiography unhistorical because biographical details are forced to fit biblical modes. On the other hand, nothing could be more historical because the literary imitation of biblical events shows how the monks and their followers viewed their lives. Considering how few outsiders ever saw the monks *in situ*, the hagiography becomes even more important.

Imitation of biblical figures did not begin with monastic hagiography but appears in the first century in the gospel of Matthew which portrays Jesus as the new Moses—an infant escaping death from a persecuting ruler, the lawgiver expounding the new dispensation on the mount (Mat. 1:13-18; 5:1-7:29). In the second century, the Martyrdom of Polycarp has it subject's death mirror that of Jesus.[7] But the words and deeds of the Desert Fathers attained such immense popularity, one can probably say that monastic hagiography created the imitation of Christ genre on the large scale.

Some examples of biblical motifs will suffice. One has already been discussed, the encounter with the devil in the desert. Another prominent motif was thaumaturgy, or miracle working. Thus, Saints Macarios and Benjamin healed the sick. Saints Amoun and Piamoun received angelic ministrations, while Saints Bessarion, Pachon and Xanthias exorcised demons. Saint Macarios the Egyptian even raised a man from the dead, but only for a few minutes to ask him a question.[8]

Lesser motifs were also used. Saint Gaddenes was miraculously saved from attack by the Jews. The burial place of Antony, like that of Moses, was unknown. Occasionally, the hagiographer announced the biblical comparisons, for example, Palladios com-

pares the monk Benjamin to Job and Paesius and Isaias to Abraham and Elijah.[9]
One biblical motif was especially popular, that of the wise teacher passing on his wisdom to a group of disciples.[10] There was in Egypt a long tradition of wisdom teaching, dating back to Ptah-hotep (ca. 2400 B.C.), a tradition no doubt preserved among the simple, Coptic-speaking monks, but here again the biblical element was decisive. The advice of many Desert Fathers sounds like material from the Book of Proverbs, while the portrait of the saintly teacher instructing his disciples mirrors that of Jesus.[11]

Not all the hagiographical elements were biblical, and many were suitable, if not unique, to life in the desert. The monks had fled the world, so there are references to their being dead to the world. Some literally walled themselves away from civilization. They immured themselves in narrow cells with only small openings for food and drink, although only minimum amounts. These places of confinement were naturally compared to tombs.[12]

Some other elements stressed life in the desert. The monks had returned to nature, so many of their miracles involved animals. Usually the monk would make a servant of a wild beast or the beast would be a witness of the monk's power. This latter motif could profitably be used to contrast the blindness of the humans who do not recognize the holy man. Occasionally the beasts are mythical, such as a basilisk or a dragon.[13] There are biblical prototypes for these miracles such as the peaceful coexistence of human and animal in the Garden of Paradise, the miracles of Elijah with the raven and Elisha with the bear, and in the New Testament of Paul with the viper. It is, however, likely that the monastic *Sitz-im-Leben* was the strongest consideration. In many cases animals were probably the only companions the hermits had.

The elements discussed so far are the more spectacular ones, but ultimately the key elements were those basic to monastic life—withdrawal, asceticism, continence and prayer. These are found throughout the hagiography.

Thus a somewhat idealistic picture emerges: the ascetic in the desert, imitating Christ and battling the world, the flesh and the devil—and this is the picture which caught the imagination of the outside world, both East and West.

But another, very disturbing element was also present right from the beginning, namely, the superiority of the monastic life.

Christianity is basically an egalitarian religion. Before God and thus in the Church there is neither Jew nor Greek, slave nor free, male nor female (Galatians 3:28); the Christian life is open to all. By the fourth century, this life open to all had taken on certain features, such as a hierarchy, a sacramental system and a communal worship. But to all of this the monks said No.

The hermits obviously lived without bishops, sacraments and liturgies, but to a great extent so did the early cenobites. Frequently they formed communities of lay brothers, none of whom was able to administer sacraments. As the hierarchical church took on the works and pomps of Roman society,[14] it became almost a threat to the monks. As Peter Brown has put it, "(The holy man) fled women and bishops,"[15] both dangers to monastic virtue. The hierarchical Church formed a part of the society which the ascetics had renounced.

As long as a live-and-let live situation existed, there were few problems. But as more and more Christians went to the desert, and as even more Christians began to consider monasticism an almost ideal Christian life, the situation changed. How could the bishops condone a mode of life which considered itself superior to almost all the bishops stood for? The answer, of course, was that they could not. Throughout the late fourth and fifth centuries the bishops, especially those of Alexandria, sought to impose their control over the monks.

The monks enjoyed immense prestige among the Christian populace, but against determined, concentrated episcopal power, there was actually little they could do. The hermits could remain alone and virtually untouched, but the ever-growing numbers of cenobites were trapped, faced with the choice of obeying or facing excommunication. They obeyed, but frequently only on the surface or begrudgingly. The hagiography reflects this situation.

The literature offers abundant examples of monastic-episcopal conflicts, with the monks' attitudes ranging from condescending to rude. Ammonius refused to receive Bishop Timothy who wished to ordain him a priest. When seven bishops had finished visiting the abbot Nathaniel, he refused to escort them as they left, saying he was dead to bishops and to the world. Arsenios told Bishop Theophilos to stop bothering him, while Pambo refused even to speak to Theophilos, telling his disciples, "If he is not edified by my silence, he will not be edified by my speech."[16] When Archibishop Athanasios wrote the life of the great Antony, he stressed that this foremost of Egyptian ascetics,

> renowned man that he was, he yet showed the profoundest respect for the Church's ministry and he wanted every cleric to be honored above himself. He was not ashamed to bow his head before bishops and priests . . . . [17]

Athanasios obviously thought that including this in Antony's *vita* might influence the more refractory monks to go along with the bishops.

Occasionally monks become bishops, an apparent solution to the problem. But two of the best-known examples, John Chrysostom and Nestorios, both bishops of Constantinople, had tempestuous episcopates and were expelled from their sees by other bishops, although not necessarily because of their monastic backgrounds.

The problem was solved when both sides realized the futility of good Christians disagreeing when both had the same goal, a better Christian life. Moderates on both sides came to the fore. The monks accepted episcopal control, but the bishops exercised this control prudently and cautiously. After the sixth century the old animosities largely disappeared. By that time, however, the monastic-episcopal opposition had become a part of the ascetics' hagiography which, as noted above, was the prime vehicle for the outside world's knowledge of the life of the desert.

Throughout the fourth century accounts of the monks trickled to the Latin West. In 336-37 the trickle became a steadily-running stream when Athanasios, expelled from his see by Arian and Melitian sympathizers, came to reside at Trier. In 340 he was again in the West, at Rome. He provided his Latin hosts with a first-hand account of the Desert Fathers. His life of Saint Antony was soon translated into Latin by Evagrios of Antioch and thus made available to a wide audience. Its many readers included the greatest of all the Latins, Augustine.[18]

Western visitors to the East, such as the Spanish nun Egeria, began to bring back more accounts, while other Easterners travelled to the West, for example, the famous hagiographer Palladios visited Rome in 405. The great scholar Jerome practised asceticism in the Syrian desert, encouraged and spread it in Rome, and in 385 settled in Bethlehem where he wrote the lives of the hermits Paul, Malchos and Hilarion. His voluminous correspondence with Roman friends provided continuous if contentious support for the ascetic movement in the West.[19] Several Roman aristocrats, such as Melania the Elder and Melania the Younger, also followed the ascetic life. Their immense social prestige gained for the movement an acceptance in influential political and ecclesiastical circles.[20]

But from the outset, monasticism encountered severe opposition from the religiously conservative West. The spectacular and undisciplined elements of desert life frightened some Western bishops, especially the Gallic ones, who saw the movement as a threat to ecclesiastical order. The presence of an ascetic and heretical group, the Priscillianites, in Gaul and Spain did nothing to allay their fears.[21]

The devotion to asceticism of the Roman aristocrats also had some negative effects since fears were raised that some families might die out for lack of progeny and that wealth would disappear as rich ascetics gave their money to the poor.[22] When the young noblewoman Blesilla died, ostensibly from the austerities imposed by her spiritual advisor Jerome, the angry Roman populace rioted against the *detestabile genus monachorum,* "the detestable race of monks."[23]

The opposition to the ascetics occasionally reached the highest levels. Both Pope Siricius (384-99) and Pope Celestine I (422-32) wrote against monasticism.[24]

But on this point, the West learned from the East. Neither monks nor bishops wanted trouble, and a rapprochement was achieved in a relatively short time. Most of the bishops recognized that monasticism was, in Victor Hugo's famous phrase, "an idea whose time had come." As the East had shown, bishops could live with moderate monasticism and asceticism. This became the pattern for the West.

John Cassian (ca. 360-435), an Eastern monk who had spent a decade in the Egyptian desert, settled near Marseilles ca. 415, founded two monasteries, and wrote rules and institutes for monks. These works were moderate in tone, simultaneously praising asceticism and ignoring or criticizing extremities. Cassian expected bishops and monks to live in harmony.[25]

Honoratus (ca. 350-429) founded a monastery on the island of Lerins off the Riviera coast. From this island came a succession of Gallic church leaders such as Hilary of Arles, Eucherius of Lyons, Vincent of Lerins, Lupus of Troyes and Caesarius of Arles.[26] Another Gaul, Paulinus of Nola, embraced the monastic life with his wife, but they did this so moderately that some other ascetics were scandalized.[27] Martin of Tours, who will be discussed in some detail below, violated his own ascetical program if he thought it would intereferre with the Christian norm of charity; for example, he usually refused to accept gifts from anyone but accepted one from a female recluse to give witness to her sanctity, fearing that a refusal might be misunderstood as a rejection of her way of life.[28]

The most striking proof of this rapprochement is the advancement of many first-generation Western monks to the episcopacy. These include Honoratus of Arles, Paulinus of Nola, Martin of Tours, Eucherius of Lyons, possibly even Patrick of Ireland.[29] On the other hand, Augustine, after becoming bishop of Hippo Regius, lived with his clergy in a semi-monastic state. The hagiographers of three famous bishops, Ambrose, Augustine and Martin, all used monastic imagery in their works.[30]

This rapprochement involved the principals, the monks and bishops, but the West followed the East in another regard. Monasticism caught the imagination of the people. The heroes of the East changed their garb to become the heroes of the West. This phenomenon may largely be credited to two men—Martin, Bishop of Tours, and his hagiographer, Sulpicius Severus.

Martin was born circa 316 in Pannonia (modern Hungary). After a career in the Roman army, he began a faithful and hazardous career in the service of the anti-Arian bishop Hilary of Poitiers. Circa 360 Martin embraced the ascetic life, practising it first at Milan, then on the island of Gallinaria, finally at Tours. His saintliness and reputation as a thaumaturge led the populace of Tours to force him to become their bishop, a situation similar to the elevations of Ambrose of Milan and Honoratus of Arles. Some bishops of the Gallo-Roman nobility resented him, claiming he was too coarse, but the people had their way. Martin held the see until his death in 397.

Almost the sole source for Martin's life is Sulpicius Severus, about whom Nora Chadwick wrote,

> As a literary artist Sulpicius has no rival in our period, and for long afterwards. It is hardly surprising that we still find difficulty in gauging just how much the beautiful and magnetic personality of St. Martin owes to the literary genius of his biographer.[31]

This paper will treat Martin and Sulpicius simultaneously.

Sulpicius (circa 363-420), an attorney, turned to the ascetic life after the death of his wife. Then in his early thirties, he came under Martin's influence. Like many a new convert, he embraced his new life wholeheartedly. Rather than work quietly on behalf of monasticism, he issued a ringing manifesto—his *Life of Martin of Tours,* supplemented by three letters and three dialogues. He made Martin the hero of the Western Christians, and he did this by portraying Martin as an Eastern ascetic. His writing dates from 395.

At the time Sulpicius wrote, important works like Athanasios' *Life of Antony* and Jerome's *Life of Paul* were known. In addition many of the episodes included in later works such as the *Lausiac History* and the *Apophthegmata Patrum* were spreading by word of mouth or by correspondence in the West. Sulpicius had his models and used them to create what was literally the first best-seller of the Christian West.

The parallels between the life of Martin and the lives of the Desert Fathers are obvious. According to Sulpicius, Martin led the simple, ascetic life, dressed poorly and had unkempt hair. He personally desired to shun the world but accepted his Christian duty, took disciples, founded the first monastery (shades of Antony) in Gaul at Marmoutier, and ministered to others as a bishop. The devil made Martin a target of his wiles, alternately threatening or cajoling him, including once appearing to him in the form of Jesus Christ. On the other hand, Martin enjoyed angelic aid, for example, the two angels protected him from the wrath of pagans whose temple he had tried to destroy. He performed exorcisms, cured the sick, converted unbelievers, and performed miracles with nature, such as overcoming a fire and commanding birds. Sulpicius even included miracles greater than those attributed to the Eastern ascetics. Martin, like Jesus himself, raised people from the dead, three to be exact.[32]

This may seem too heavy-handed to the reader, but Sulpicius, taking no chances, went even further.

He wrote a dialogue entitled *Postumianus*. Postumianus, a Gallo-Roman, spent some time in Egypt among the desert monks. He returned to Gaul and recounted for his friends the fantastic and fascinating adventures of the Eastern monks. But this is all just to entice the reader. It is a lead-in to the real topic: Martin.

After Postumianus had finished his tales, Sulpicius replied,

... when I was listening just now with the greatest interest to what you were telling us about the miracles of those holy men, my mind kept going back to my Martin, though I said nothing; and I could not help noticing that whereas each of your Egyptians performed one kind of miracle, this one man of ours did more than all they did between them. You certainly told us some very remarkable things but—if I may say so without offence to these holy men—there was absolutely nothing that I heard from you in which Martin was not their equal.[33]

Sulpicius then recounts the wonderful deeds of Martin to prove this point.

One of the most striking points of Sulpicius' writing is his hostile attitude towards the Gallic bishops, most of whom apparently opposed Martin. They were, as a group, noblemen, proud of their heritage and resentful of this Pannonian soldier. But, significantly, Sulpicius writes against their shortsightedness in failing to recognize Martin's personal sanctity and the importance of the ascetic-monastic way of life. He does not write against the episcopacy as such. Indeed, his hero is a bishop. The question for the ascetics and their sympathizers was not whether to be a bishop but rather what kind of bishop.

Sulpicius' *Life of Martin* was literary dynamite.[34] It was read throughout Gaul. Paulinus of Nola spread it in Italy, and the Roman booksellers "looked upon it as a record profitmaker because nothing sold more quickly or fetched a better price."[35] British tradition says that a bishop Ninian (ca. 400) named his church in southern Scotland after Martin.[36] The book went to Ireland where it became the ultimate source of the immense popularity of the name Martin.[37] Postumianus recounted that it was read in Latin North Africa and in Greek Alexandria, and—the *coup de grace*—the monks in the Egyptian desert, upon learning that Postumianus was a friend of Sulpicius, begged him to have Sulpicius write more about Martin![38] A less spectacular but equally significant proof of the book's success is that in the next century, Gregory, Bishop of Tours, descendant of a noble Gallo-Roman family with many bishops in its lineage, made the miraculous activities of the long-deceased Martin—and of his relics—a major emphasis in his *History of the Franks.*[39]

Thus it would seem that Eastern monasticism made a successful journey to the West and that the lessons learned in the East were learned in the West. Moderate, essentially cenobitic monasticism in harmony with the episcopate eventually became the standard, even to the point where the greatest Western monastic founder, Benedict, could suggest that bishops intervene to reform life in a corrupted monastery.[40]

It would also seem that this account of the monastic journey should come to an end. But, ironically, at the same time the rapprochement was being effected in the Western Church, two new peoples entered that Church and unwittingly gave added life to the primitive forms of Eastern monasticism, seemingly at the moment of their death.

The Irish became Christian in the fifth century and the Anglo-Saxons at the end of the sixth and throughout the seventh century. These peoples had never been part of the Roman Empire and became Christians while still culturally barbarians. They belonged to heroic societies, societies in which individual prowess counted for more than offices or titles. Their folk heroes were men like Cuchulainn and Beowulf, who singlehandedly battled armies and dragons. Among these peoples, desert monasticism in its more spectacular forms witnessed a remarkable revival. Among the Irish, Columbanus imposed daily fasting upon his monks, and monastic plows were drawn not by draft animals but by the brothers.[41] Among the English, Cuthbert had a cell on Farne island, "a hut surrounded by an embankment so high that he could see nothing but the heavens for which he longed so ardently,"[42] but which also offered virtually no protection from the North Sea storms.

In the insular hagiography it is occasionally difficult to distinguish the pagan from the Christian elements. How much is the saint the independent, individualistic Egyptian ascetic facing the devil or how much is he a Christian Beowulf facing the dragon, a common image for the devil? The exact relation may be undeterminable, and even perhaps unimportant. The key point is that the pagan tradition provided the cultural framework for the revival of primitive monasticism.

A second problem in the hagiography is whether the Irish and Anglo-Saxons modelled their hagiography after the Easterners or after Western writers such as Sulpicius Severus. Episodes which are common to both traditions obviously could have come from either, but all that would actually prove is that the

Western writers were the filter of the Eastern tradition. There are, however, clear proofs of Eastern influence. Among the Irish, parts of Adamnan's *Life of Columba* correspond to the Latin version of the *Life of Antony,* occasionally verbatim;[43] an anonymous Irish commentator on Luke's gospel spoke of "monks who follow the rule of the desert."[44] Among the English, Saints Antony and Paul appear on the Ruthwell Cross, one of the monuments of Anglo-Saxon art; the *Life of Guthlac* tells how two demons tried to tempt him by offering to teach him the way of life of "those renowned monks who dwelt in Egypt...."[45] More than just the famous Eastern saints were known. The sixth-century Spanish bishop Martin of Braga translated some of the sayings of the Desert Fathers into Latin; the connections between Spain and the British Isles in the Early Middle Ages were strong.[46]

Familiar hagiographical elements reappear. The Irish saint Columba or Colmcille was attacked by demons but aided by angels, he performed healings and exorcisms, and worked miracles with animals and the forces of nature.[47] Saint Kevin of Glendalough sought refuge from the world in a secluded valley where he too endured demonic assaults, enjoyed angelic ministrations and lived in harmony with the wild animals. He came in contact with people infrequently, but frequently enough to perform an assortment of miracles such as killing sheep to feed starving people but finding that his flock had not diminished in size. Eventually his fame for sanctity brought him disciples and he agreed to found a community, one of the most famous in Ireland.[48] Similar examples can be found in the lives of many other Irish saints.

But Ireland was not Egypt, and the Irish hagiography combines unique and traditional elements. For example Ireland is an island, and its people have always lived close to the sea. To the Early Christian Irish, the wild, empty waters of the North Atlantic appeared just as lonely and forbidding as the desert did to the Egyptians. One of the great Irish saints, Brendan the Navigator, took some disciples and set sail on the barren, endless ocean in search of the Blessed Isles, an obvious re-enactment of the Egyptians' withdrawal to the desert in search of the heavenly life. But Brendan also re-enacted the voyage of the pagan hero Bran who searched the seas for the Happy Otherworld.[49] Thus the life of the saint merged the pagan and Eastern traditions.

Another example of the Irish combination of the traditional and the unique is the life of Saint Bridgit. Pagan Celtic law gave women a higher status than they enjoyed in Christian Roman society. When monasticism rose to prominence in Ireland, there was nothing to prevent a woman from becoming one of its leaders. There were Eastern women ascetics such as Pelagia the Harlot, but they paled in importance beside the great men. Bridgit, on the other hand, came to be regarded with Saints Patrick and Columcille as one of the three pillars of the Irish Church. Yet the way in which the unique—a woman—became acceptable was to become the familiar—an Eastern monk. The traditions about Bridgit leave much to be desired historically, but hagiographically they fill the bill: Bridgit was a virgin, threatened by pagans, worked miracles with animals and natural forces (including hanging her cloak on a ray of sunlight), and became a monastic founder at Kildare.[50]

The Irish evangelized the English in Northumbria, and they transferred their enthusiasm for the desert saints to their converts. Most English hagiography was written after the Synod of Whitby (664) when the Northumbrians decided to follow the formal, organized Roman way of Christianity. Consequently the English hagiographers do not emphasize the more primitive ascetic traits of their subjects as much as the Irish, but enough information survives to show that the old ways had their day among the English, too.

A few examples will suffice. According to the historian Bede, Cuthbert was a hermit, lived on a deserted island, expelled demons, performed miracles with animals and natural forces, attracted others by his sanctity and was forced by popular demand to become a bishop.[51] Chad was able to work miracles with natural forces, stopping a storm with his prayers.[52] Guthlac routed demons by citing Psalm 67:2, the same verse used by Antony to rout demons.[53]

Eventually the inevitable happened. The hierarchically-ordered Roman way came to dominate both the English and Irish churches. In the name of discipline, individualism was stamped out. Hermits practically disappeared, while cenobites followed the moderate, stable Benedictine way. The asceticism of the Desert Fathers, transplanted to the North, had finally become a thing of the past. By the late eighth century the tales of primitive monasticism had become what they still are today—more romance than reality.

This account will close with two citations, an eloquent one from a modern writer and a simple but artful one from an Early Medieval writer. Each citation demonstrates, in its own way, the extensive influence of the lives of the Eastern monks on the West.

The first is from Brendan Lehane.

> So Christianity penetrated to Ireland. It came across the sea from Gaul, and across the narrower channel from Wales. It was not a predestined trip. No anchorite in the desert could have imagined his image and example travelling over land and sea, through the wavy plains of desert and the foetid stalls of Alexandria, across the Mediterranean in vulnerable ships that stopped sailing in October because of winter squalls, through marbled complacent Rome and the crushed and clamorous markets of Marseilles, across the terraced vineyards of Provence and the Massif, down to the starker, colder plains of northern France and finally into the foggy unknown of the English channel—to ignite, after four thousand miles, an isolated culture set in the northern seas. No one could have imagined it, but so it happened.[54]

The second is from the Venerable Bede, an English monk and historian (673-735), an ardent supporter of the Roman way and of moderate monasticism, yet one who could still appreciate the heroism and individuality of primitive monasticism. Bede tells this story of the monk Drycthelm.

> This man was given a more secluded dwelling in the monastery, so that he could devote himself more freely to the service of his Maker in unbroken prayer. And since this place stands on the bank of a river, he often used to enter it for severe bodily penance, and plunge repeatedly beneath the water while he recited psalms and prayers for as long as he could endure it, standing motionless with the water up to his loins and some-

times to his neck. When he returned to shore, he never removed his dripping, chilly garments, but let them warm and dry on his body. And in winter, when the half-broken cakes of ice were swirling around him which he had broken to make a place to stand and dip himself in the water, those who saw him used to say: 'Brother Drycthelm, it is wonderful how you can manage to bear such bitter cold.' To which he, being a man of simple disposition and self-restraint, would reply simply, 'I have known it colder.'[55]

NOTES

1. Because of the popular nature of the Tuohy Chair lectures, this paper will, as much as possible, cite material in English. It will also try to cite widely-available editions, such as Rex Warner's translation of Augustine's *Confessions,* or Leo Sherley-Price's translation of Bede.

2. A reliable account of Eastern monasticism is Derwas Chitty, *The Desert a City* (London, 1966). Many primary sources are in English. Those used for this paper are Athanasios, *The Life of Saint Antony,* trans. Robert Meyer, Ancient Christian Writers 10 (Westminster, Md., 1950)—hereafter cited *LSA*; Palladios, *The Lausiac History,* trans. Robert Meyer, ACW 34 (Westminster, Md., 1965)—hereafter cited *LH; The Sayings of the Desert Fathers (Apophthegmata Patrum): the Alphabetical Collection,* trans. Benedicta Ward (London, 1975)—hereafter cited *SDF*; Jerome, *The Life of St. Paul the First Hermit,* trans. Helen Waddell in *The Desert Fathers* (London, 1960), pp. 41-53—hereafter cited *Paul.*

3. Professor Sullivan read his paper, "The Origins of Monasticism— Towards a Revision," at the Second Mid-Atlantic States Conference on Patristic, Mediaeval and Renaissance Studies, Villanova University, 1 October 1977. He has kindly given this writer a copy of the paper.

4. *LSA* 3; p. 20.

5. *Paul, passim;* the most recent discussion of Jerome as biographer is by J. N. D. Kelly, *Jerome: His Life, Writings, and Controversies* (New York, 1975(, ch. xvi, "Propagandist History," pp. 168-78.

6. Arnaldo Momigliano, "Christianity and the Decline of the Roman Empire," in *The Conflict between Paganism and Christianity in the Fourth Century,* ed. A. Momigliano (Oxford, 1963), p. 11.

7. *Martyrdom of Polycarp,* trans. J. A. Kleist, ACW 6 (Westminster, Md., 1948), 90-101.

8. *LH* 12:1-2; 18:19-21; 8:6; 31:1-2; 23:4-6; pp. 48, 63-64, 43, 90-91, 82-83; *SDF* Bessarion 5, Xanthias 2, Macarios the Great 7; pp. 35, 133-34, 108-9.

9. *LH* 50, 13:1-2, 14:4; pp. 132, 47-48, 50; *LSA* 92, p. 96. The remains of Saint Antony were discovered in 561; cf. *LSA* p. 132, n. 298.

10. *SDF, passim.*

11. Peter Brown has pointed out the social significance of this folk wisdom: "In these *Sayings,* the peasantry of Egypt spoke for the first time to the civilized world," *The World of Late Antiquity* (London, 1971), p. 100.

12. *LH* 5, 28; pp. 36, 88. Antony actually lived in a tomb; *LSA* 8; p. 26.

13. *LH* 17:6-9 (in which Macarios of Egypt aids a woman who has been turned into a horse), 18:9; pp. 56-57, 60-61; *SDF* Ammonas 2; p. 22.

14. Brown, *World of Late Antiquity,* ch. vii, "The Conversion of Christianity," pp. 82-95.

15. Brown, "The Rise of the Holy Man in Late Antiquity," *Journal of Roman Studies* 61(1971) 92.

16. *LH* 11:1-3, 16:3-4; pp. 46-47, 52-53; *SDF* Arsenios 7, Theophilos 2; pp. 8, 69.

17. *LSA* 67; p. 76.

18. Augustine, *Confessions,* viii, 6, trans. Rex Warner (New York, 1963), pp. 171-72.

19. Kelly, *Jerome,* pp. 179-94.

20. Anne Yarbrough, "Christianization in the Fourth Century: the Example of Roman Women," *Church History* 45 (1976) 149-65.

21. Henry Chadwick, *Priscillian of Avila: the Occult and Charismatic in the Early Church* (Oxford, 1976).

22. Yarbrough, "Christianization."

23. Kelly, *Jerome,* p. 108.

24. For Siricius, cf. Joseph T. Lienhard, S. J., *Paulinus of Nola and Early Western Monasticism* (Cologne-Bonn, 1977), pp. 119-23; for Celestine, cf. R. P. C. Hanson, *Saint Patrick: His Origins and Career* (Oxford, 1968), p. 141.

25. The standard account of Cassian's career is Owen Chadwick, *John Cassian,* 2nd ed. (Cambridge, 1968).

26. Nora Chadwick, *Poetry and Letters in Early Christian Gaul* (London, 1955), ch. vi, "Foundations of Western Monasticism, the Monastery of Lerins," pp. 142-69.

27. Ibid., pp. 72-73.

28. Sulpicius Severus, *Dialogue* 2, xii, trans. F.R. Hoare, *The Western Fathers* (London, 1954), p. 117-18.

29. Hanson, *Saint Patrick,* discusses the evidence for Patrick's relations with monasticism, pp. 140-58.

30. Philip Rousseau, "The Spiritual Authority of the 'Monk-Bishop': Eastern Elements in Some Western Hagiography of the Fourth and Fifth Centuries," *Journal of Theological Studies,* n.s., 22 (1971) 380-419.

31. N. Chadwick, *Poetry and Letters,* p. 121.

32. These examples are taken from various parts of Sulpicius' works and can almost be cited *passim*. The most interesting one, the devil appearing to Martin in the form of Jesus, is from *The Life of Martin of Tours,* 24, *The Western Fathers,* pp. 40-41.

33. Sulpicius Severus, *Dialogue* 1, xxiv, *The Western Fathers,* pp. 96-97.

34. An eminent contemporary scholar could write, "Probably no-one has ever reached the final page of Sulpicius Severus without regrets," Nora Chadwick, *Poetry and Letters,* p. 121. Sulpicius' story of Martin's dividing his soldier's cloak with his sword and giving half to a beggar is still one of the famous tales of saints; cf. *Life of Martin* 3, The Western Fathers, pp. 14-15.

35. Sulpicius Severus, *Dialogue* 1, xxiii, *The Western Fathers,* p. 96.

36. Bede, *A History of the English Church and People,* iii. 4, trans. Leo Serley-Price, rev. R. E. Latham (Baltimore, 1968), p. 146. But in spite of Bede's witness, the historical traditions about Ninian are vague.

37. Aubrey Gwynn, "The Cult of St. Martin in Ireland, *Irish Ecclesiastical Record* 105 (1966) 353-64.

38. Sulpicius Severus, *Dialogue* 1, xxiii, *The Western Fathers,* p. 96.

39. Gregory of Tours, *The History of the Franks,* trans. Lewis Thorpe (Baltimore, 1974). A brief glance at the index (pp. 605-710) will indicate how much more frequently Martin is mentioned than many of Gregory's contemporaries about whom the book is supposed to be. For Gregory, Martin was as alive as all of them.

40. *The Rule of St. Benedict,* ch. 64, trans. Anthony Meisel & M. L. del Mastro (Garden City, N.Y., 1975), p. 99.

41. John Ryan, *Irish Monasticism: Origins and Early Development* (Shannon, 1972), pp. 360-64, 399-401.

42. Bede, *History of the English Church,* iv. 28, p. 262.

43. Adamnan, *Life of Columba,* in *Adomnan's (sic) Life of Columba,* ed. & trans. A. O. Anderson (London, 1961), *inter alia* p. 518, n. 10; p. 520, n. 3; p. 522, n. 2.

44. *Commentarius in Lucam,* iv. 1, ed. Joseph F. Kelly, *Corpus Christianorum series latina* 108 C (Turnholt, 1974), 29.

45. Felix, *Life of Guthlac* 30, trans. Clinton Albertson, *Anglo-Saxon Saints and Heroes* (Bronx, N.Y., 1967), p. 187; for references to Antony and Paul on the Ruthwell Cross, p. 47, n. 21.

46. Martin of Braga, *Sayings of the Desert Fathers,* trans. Claude Barlow, Fathers of the Church 62 (Washington, D.C., 1969), 17-34; for connections between Spain and the British Isles, cf. Jocelyn Hillgarth, "Old Ireland and Visigothic Spain," in *Old Ireland,* ed. Robert E. McNally (Bronx, N.Y., 1965), pp. 200-27, and "The Liturgical Trade Route: Egypt to Ireland (500 to 700 A.D.)" by J. H. Crehan, S. J., forthcoming in *Studia Patristica.*

47. Adamnan, *Life of Columba,* I.1, III.8, II.11, III.23, II.34; pp. 195, 481, 349-51, 523-35, 407.

48. Some of these early traditions are preserved in a late (eleventh century) life of Kevin, translated by Charles Plummer, *Lives of Irish Saints,* 2 (Oxford, 1922), 121-26.

49. *The Voyage of Saint Brendan,* trans. J. F. Webb, in *Lives of the Saints* (Baltimore, 1965), pp. 31-68; "The Voyage of Bran," trans. T. P. Cross & C. H. Slover, *Ancient Irish Tales* (Dublin, 1936), pp. 588-95.

50. There is no English translation of the earliest life of Bridgit, that of Cogitosus, *Sanctae Brigidae Virginis Vita, Patrologia Latina* 72, 775-790.

51. Bede, *History of the English Church,* iv. 27-29, pp. 259-65; *Life of Cuthbert* in *Lives of the Saints,* pp. 69-129.

52. Bede, *History of the English Church,* iv. 3, p. 211.

53. Felix, *Life of Guthlac* 34, *Anglo-Saxon Saints and Heroes,* p. 193.

54. Brendan Lehane, *The Quest of Three Abbots* (London, 1968), p. 22.

55. Bede, *History of the English Church,* v. 12, p. 294.

THE SOCIAL ETHOS OF THE ORTHODOX CHURCH
by
DEMETRIOS J. CONSTANTELOS

Should the Christian Church engage in social and political action? Is social action antithetical to spirituality and religious functions? There are no simple answers that can fully satisfy such questions. The fact is that genuine spirituality and faithful witness demand discretion with respect to social problems and political issues, with respect to times and circumstances. The attitude of the Church should correspond to the mandate of her Master and Lord. What the Lord taught, the Church must also teach; what the Master did, the Church must also do. The Lord was the servant of all persons but especially the poor and the oppressed, the sick and the alienated. The Church, imitating her Master, should be prophetic and the herald of God's righteousness, she must assume the servant-role and she must be prepared to risk even martyrdom and death in order to defend the teachings and imitate the Master's role.

The question is: does the Orthodox Church have a social ethos? The answer is emphatically yes. But, then, what are its sources, its theological presuppositions, and the manifestations of its practical application? In the present article we are concerned with the social and moral thought of Orthodoxy—not its application, even though we could illustrate much with concrete examples of Orthodoxy's experience in the world.

The social ethos of the Orthodox Church emanates from the concept of the new commandment of *agape*. And *agape* among men is the imitation of God's love for all persons. God manifested His *agape* in the God-made-man event of the incarnation of the eternal Logos-the Christ. From a theological point of view and from a historical perspective, the social character of the Church is the application of the doctrinal teaching concerning God and human beings, and human beings with respect to their social relations. Social ethos, as the result of applied ethics, is solidly based on theological presuppositions.

The Orthodox tradition emphasizes that one rejoins God by possessing an ecstatic love for the Divine Being and by expressing a similar sense of love for God's supreme being. It is by energetic love for God and human persons that one can attain a state of *theosis*, "possessing the love and knowledge of God."[1]

In the last analysis, the social ethos is rooted in christological, soteriological, anthropological, ecclesiological, eucharistic, and eschatological presuppostions. It was upon these theological categories that the rich social involvement of the early and medieval church was built.

The *christological* doctrine was formulated on the basis of the earthly activity of the God-man *Christos*, who becomes the inspiration of the social activity of the individual believer as well as for the social response of the Christian Ecclesia as an institution. There is no justice proper, no virtue, except christocentric virtue. "Love one another as I have loved you" or "A New Commandment I am giving unto you—to love one another as I have loved you."[2]

Thus the Christian community is charged with the responsibility and the task of applied *agape* because its founder was the personification of *agape*, and he was socially involved and deeply concerned with the lowly, the unloved, and the disregarded members of society. What Christ did, the Church must do. The Ecclesia is an extension of the perpetuation of the person and the work of Christ here on earth. All people must be drawn to God, and it is through vigorous activity that all people, rich and poor, wise and foolish, young and old, will unite in the presence of God. The practice of love becomes a universal unitive force for God and humans. "To turn your back against even one poor individual is to show contempt toward all humanity. To refuse assistance to one indigent person is to commit injustice to all humanity because man is a microcosm and the convergence of all humanity,"[3] as Patriarch George Scholarios wrote in the fifteenth century.

The Eternal Logos, Christ, divested himself of supernatural glory in order to reach out and direct the earthly to eternal glory. God walked among humans that human beings may walk with God. Or in the classic words of Irenaeos and Athanasios who emphasized that "the Lord . . . came to us not as He could, but as we could see Him" and that the Lord "being God, later He became man, in order that we may become gods."[4] This kind of patristic thought has been taken very seriously by the Orthodox and has contributed immensely to the formation of their social ethos. Notwithstanding the ultimate supernatural destiny of the Ecclesia, the Christian Community cannot divorce itself from this world but, as Christ did, it too must do and invade, and penetrate into the present world "doing good." The Logos became human in order to announce release to the captives, to recover the sight of the blind, to set at liberty those who have been enslaved, to proclaim that the time of God has arrived.[5] God became human, thus nothing human should be foreign to the Church.

On this basis then, the Church, as an organism and organization of Christ and through its affinity with Christ's earthly ministry, emulates the work of the Lord. Thus, the social thought of Orthodoxy assumes a theanthropic character which is based furthermore not only on christology but on the theological teaching of the Fatherhood of God. "God so loved the world that He gave His only Son, that whoever believes in Him should not perish but have eternal life."[6] Christ called God Father and fulfilled God's will. On account of man's relationship to Christ the man, those who supplicate the same God and acknowledge God as common Father, the Creator of the Cosmos and of all humans, become automatically charged with social obligations to their fellow humans. In their faith in God they accept also God's paternity over the entire *oecumene.* The paternity of God obliges all—healthy and sick, slaves and free, blacks and whites, kings and soldiers, civilized and barbarians to effect an earthly kingdom of God—to paraphrase St. Gregory Nazianzenos.[7]

Such a creed energizes an impulse for social action whose immediate objective is the betterment of human society here on earth as a dim reflection of the perfect *koinonia* in Heaven. Because of God's philanthropy and concern for man, God's plan (economy), for man's redemption, is defined by the Byzantine theologian Nicholas Kabasilas as *Compassion* or *Mercy*.[8] Man's earthly activity then must be one of continuous compassion toward all men.

In imitation of God's two-way involvement in human history, humans must also manifest their concern for their fellow humans in two manners which correspond to humanity's dual nature, the physical and the spiritual. One imitates God's philanthropy when one feeds the hungry, gives a drink to the stranger, visits the sick, redeems the prisoners, and buries the dead who have no one to bury them. To these seven physical activities correspond seven spiritual concerns: to console those in sorrow, to give advice to the timid and undecided, to teach the ignorant, to guide the sinner and to forgive the fallen, to be patient with the rude and insolent, and lastly to pray for all, in the words of George Scholarios.[9]

The social thought of the Greek fathers, who laid the ground and who expressed the life and creed of Orthodox theology, is linked with the social aspects of soteriology since their ultimate concern was the salvation of the individual soul as well as the redemption of the Christian community. In the history of the Greek people, the Church has performed a double function; it has concerned itself with the eternal salvation of human souls, but it has also served as the agency of social improvement and physical survival. Its social posture has often given meaning and direction to the social thought and action of the individual as well as of the state. This, in particular, is evident during the last two centuries of the medieval era when the Church was the only hope for the overwhelming majority of the populace, as well as during the four centuries of captivity under the Ottoman Empire, and even in modern times. It is on this basis that one can understand why an Archbishop can serve as an ethnarch or get involved in secular aspects of his people's life.

It is not only the principle of humanitarian social obligations toward the indigent that Orthodox theology teaches but also the theological concept that one is called by the creator to become a *synergos* of God, a collaborator for the completion of God's work, both in ONE's own person and in the persons united in Christ's body—the Church. And God's work is not only spiritual—it embraces all aspects of human life.

It is impossible to disassociate anthropology from a discussion concerning the social ethos of the Orthodox Church. Humans are viewed as the image and likeness of God, whose ultimate goal is eternal life in God (*theosis*). Their earthly destiny is to become holy because their God is Holy, and their eternal goal is to achieve deification (*theosis*) because they are children of God. Nevertheless, holiness and moral perfection are evolutionary elements, not achievements *per se* to be accomplished here on earth. Cultivation and moral development are pursued through spiritual exercise, prayer, and contemplation, but also through the creative use of man's will and freedom in the service of God and God's people through "faith active in love"—*agape* in *diakonia.*[10]

Orthodox theology sees dynamic love as one's immediate goal here on earth in order that one may gain ultimately the crown of glory. The moral perfection of the human being commences from the earthly and is to be pursued in association with and in service to God's people, while our terminal *theosis* will be achieved in the kingdom to come. The human principle occupies a central position in the thought and social concern of the Church. The entire social thought of Orthodoxy is based on the recognition of one's worth, on the respect, love consideration, and anxiety for one's destiny whatsoever one's social standing, state position, origins, or race may be. As the object of the love of God, each person must be the most important object of anxiety and service for the Church for he or she is a microcosm of all humanity.

John Chrysostom's view of the human being has exerted a telling influence on Orthodox moral theology. Chrysostom writes: "I have no contempt for any person because every person is most worthy of attention as one of God's creatures. Even if one is a slave one is not despicable for I am not looking at social ranks but for virtue. I am looking neither for a master nor for a slave but for the human person for whom the heavens opened, the sun shines, the moon races on, the air fills all, the fountains give their water, the sea spreads out, for whom, indeed, the only begotten Son of God became man. My master was slaughtered and shed his blood for man and who am I to overlook man? How could I be forgiven?"[11]

God's creation constitutes a single and whole entity. There is no drastic separation between the earthly Ecclesia and the supernatural community because both constitute the whole of God's creation. God's creation is all-encompassing, and the physical is linked with the metaphysical. It is for this reason that in Orthodox theology the supernatural aspect of the Church is not treated in isolation from the physical or visible Church; and that the saints, the fathers, the martyrs, and other holy men of the past are in fact contemporaries. The present incorporates the past and anticipates the future. Their Church is our Church and our Church is in a direct historical continuity with their Church.

The unity and continuity of the social ethos of present day Orthodoxy with that of the past is very real. Orthodoxy's conception of history is linear and Orthodoxy recognizes no major disruptions. It takes history very seriously and theology is both determined and conditioned by history. In fact, there is no theology *per se*, but only historical theology. It is for this reason that the Orthodox have high regard for decisions, examples, and illustrations from history. It is because of their historical conscience that the Orthodox appeal to the authority of tradition, the mind of the Fathers, the decisions of ecumenical councils—the holiness and the experience of the past. The past lives in the present and it will continue to live as long as human beings will live. This means that the social ethos of the Church is also the result of her ecclesiological perception.

The ecclesiological concept concerning the Church as the Household or Family of God presupposes that Church members accept *agape* or *philanthropia* as a common denominator, freely flowing, expecting nothing in return. It is this type of unmerited philanthropy that made Christian love transcend the boundaries of ancient Greco-Roman humanism and the self-oriented Jewish liberality. It transformed an anthropocentric and limited humanism into a theocentric and ecumenical philanthropy. Of course not all Christians, either clergy or laity, respond to this model of social thought and concern, but overwhelming evidence confirms that there were and there are numerous believers who have adopted and transmitted this ideal in their daily life. To help the poor, visit the sick, guide the lost, receive the stranger, look after the lepers, protect the orphans and stand publicly for social justice are types of the love leading to ultimate sanctification.[12] Whether wealthy or poor, prominent or humble, healthy or sick, they receive communion from the same chalice—a social event in itself which confirms and seals their fellowship in God and their social and mutual reconciliation.

The Eucharist is offered to the faithful from the same cup. Receiving from the same chalice becomes the supreme socializing experience which makes public association feasible. If the rich and prominent receive the Eucharist from a common altar with the poor and the socially destitute, it is not difficult for them to sympathize with and be of assistance to others.

In the Eucharistic Communion there is real communion of life which extends to eternity. Holy Communion as actual union with Christ becomes a foundation stone and a springboard of social interest and welfare preparing for an eternal fellowship.[13] This thought of the Church was expressed centuries ago by John of Damascus who wrote of Holy Communion as a union of the faithful with the divinity of Christ, "an actual communion because through it we share in His flesh and His divinity." "Yes," he wrote, "we have communion and are united with one another through it. For since we partake of one bread, we all become one body of Christ and one blood, and members one of another, being of one body with Christ."[14]

The social ethos of the Orthodox community derives much of its strength from Eucharistic theology because it views in the act of Holy Communion not only participation in the Body of Christ but also a dynamic symbol of the unity and spiritual reciprocity of Christ's disciples. This unity signalizes mutual opportunities and responsibilities. As the common chalice becomes a public spiritual feast, likewise it serves as a common ground for social thought and activity. As all the faithful are invited to the same spiritual feast, likewise all are summoned to respond to the call for the betterment of the social order here and its perfection in the hereafter. The Church stresses the importance of values for this life which will be fully realized in the life to come. It is the *continuum* that exists between time and eternity, between the physical and the metaphysical, between the Church militant and the Church triumphant that makes eschatology a great source for the development of social thought in Christian Orthodoxy. They are intricately related. On account of this mutuality the social ethos of Orthodoxy is greatly determined by the vivid eschatological expectations and apocalyptic tendencies. The study of every major Greek Father reveals that his social thought was determined by the eschatological creed.

The frequently eschatological sermons which we find in the writings of the Church are of dual significance. They reveal prevailing social conditions but also the concern and the invitation to all the faithful for moral and social self-improvement through the practice of good works. Charity, alms, and virtuous deeds were very popular themes for sermons as they are today. The same virtues, however, give the faithful the characteristic tone of their daily existence. Great churchmen such as Basil, who washed the feet of lepers in his own hospital in Caesaria, or John the Eleemon, who built seven hospitals in Alexandria, or Patriarch Athanasios I of Constantinople, who organized food distribution and common meals in the early 14th century, or Theoleptos of Philadelphia, who took up the defence of his city against the enemy, interpreted their lives in terms of the teachings and life of Christ.[15] The Church Fathers who set the example and laid the foundations of the Church's social ethos were not other worldly beings but down to earth, concrete men who saw theology and life as two interrelated halves of a single whole.

Being in Christ means an everyday life which expresses the application of the commandments of love and sacrifice and a reflection of divine philanthropia toward all—Christians and non-Christians alike. It is for this reason that the Greek Church has embraced and consecrated the totality of the state and its concerns. The Church is the new Ark in which everybody can find assistance. The Church is not a community of saints for the service of saints, but a tender mother who invites all to her breasts to feed and receive strength for the great pilgrimage to eternity. Furthermore, the Church is viewed not as a museum of saints but as the great hospital open to all in need of healing. As the eternal Kingdom of God is opened and prepared to receive all creation in an ultimate unity, the earthly kingdom, that is, the Ecclesia, is available to those exerting their efforts to serve and embrace all. Thus the ministry of love becomes the hallmark of the Church.

The pursuit of the faithful to achieve entrance into the Eternal Kingdom determines their social ethos for they are instructed to see a continuity between the earthly reality with their future state of being. Their frame of reference is once again Christ, who did not divide the temporal from the eternal. The Church triumphant and the Church militant are two aspects of the entire Ecclesia. In full agreement with the Biblical account, the hope for rewards unseen determines their social behavior. In Christ's earthly Kingdom one becomes a new creation. The new creation evolves here on earth and follows a process of perfection which will reach its apogee in the kingdom to come. In the earthly kingdom one joins "a society in the process of deification" as St. Gregory Palamas has put it.[16] This process is a social one because deification is intended for all who join the new creation. Thus, in the long history of the Church there were many who developed a deep community interest and who believed that ultimate moral perfection begins in our social relations.

Nevertheless, the tendency of Christian Orthodoxy to emphasize the values of the eternal Kingdom did not dissipate devotion to social obligations. The Church stressed the interrelationship between duties to others with the apocalyptic expectations of the other world. One's earthly life must be regulated according to the relations one wants to establish with God in God's eternal kingdom. To make an adjustment after departure is humanly uncertain. Thus, reminding of the value of time and the limitations of our knowledge concerning our earthly existence as well as of God's final judgment has been a popular topic for sermons and admonitions. As St. Photios, the great Patriarch and scholar of the ninth century admonished: "Let us study death before death so that we may live after death."[17] The event of death becomes central to ethics because it shows that humanity belongs to eternal life and provides hope for betterment on earth as well as assurance for eternity. Long before Photios, Saint Irenaeos wrote that "the task of the Christian is nothing but to study how to die."[18]

In the course of history very frequently the Church has served as the champion of social justice, and the protector of the needy and the oppressed. There have been many remarkable churchmen who have expressed a deep interest for the fate of the poor and the persecuted; who have championed social justice; who have castigated the abuse of wealth and the exploitation of the poor. Personal property is not strictly personal but a trust which God has given to the owner. Some, such as John Chrysostom, Theodore Metochites, Adamantios Koraes, or Nicholas Psaroudakis have advocated social involvement rather than an eremitic or monastic life because social concern provides greater opportunities for the realization of the Christian ideal.

In speaking of social ethics the Church does not mean merely the contribution of money or goods to those in need. Under the term social ethics all services that can be rendered freely to anyone in need of assistance are included, from what is called "charity" to the professional services of physicians, lawyers, civil servants, and especially public hospitality and relief. The Church urges all those who can to give their money, their goods, their talents, their knowledge, their advice, and their services generally to all who stand in need of them—all poor are Christ's and as long as they do it to them they do it to Christ.

The Church, as the conscience of Christ's Gospel, plays an important role in bringing the two extremes of rich and poor together by emphasizing the significance of religious values. And religion is not isolated into a department of the state's or society's life but it is accepted as an all-encompassing way of life. The Church is both the Kingdom of God and a *politeuma*, a nationhood, an indivisible entity which has its feet firmly planted on earth and its hands stretched out like an anchor of hope, to God's eternal kingdom. As a *politeuma*, the Church is concerned with political as well as social problems.

The Church emphasizes the application of social philanthropy and private charity on other than religious grounds. Poverty and distress are often the result of our inhumanity to one another. Thus the Church appeals for the practice of public philanthropy not simply for the salvation of one's soul, nor to please God, but in order to fulfill an act of natural justice because many poor people are victims of the tyranny and the exploitation of others. As St. Photios wrote: "Do not overlook the poor and let not his tattered rags incite you to contempt, but let them rather move you to pity your fellow-creatures. For he is also a man, a creature of God, clothed in flesh like yourself, and perchance in his spiritual virtue mirroring the common Creator more than you do. Nature has not made him indigent in this way, but it is the tyranny of his neighbors that has reduced either him or his parents to indigence, while our lack of pity and compassion has maintained or even aggravated his poverty."[19]

Admittedly Orthodox theologians and churchmen today seldom make specific proposals in the realm of social action to change the social structure and remedy the evils of their society. The most frequent call against social injustices is a call to repentance, an indication that the Church expects the unjust and wealthy to initiate action by themselves without coercion from the state or other authorities. Orthodox theology views human nature as a synthetic whole in which all drives and impulses of man must become subject to the control of higher values, all of which derive from God and must serve God's people.[20] It is primarily concerned with a renewal of the inner life of each individual person. It is through renewed persons that the moral life of society is transformed. And a renewed society possesses the potential of renewing the whole state and the whole world for "a little leaven leavens all the dough."[21] While this is true, it is not the whole truth. Those Orthodox theologians who believe in the close relationship between spirituality and involvement remind us that the Orthodox Church has a social ethos which is the result of the Church's involvement in history. Thus, if some Orthodox Churches today stress only spirituality and quietude, refusing to get involved, they simply betray the social ethos of their Church in history.

NOTES

1. Maximos the Confessor, "Capita de Capita de Charitate I:23-27," *PG* 90:965A-C; Photios, "Homily 33.8," ed. S. Aristarches, *Photiou Logoi kai Homiliai,* 1 (Constantinople, 1900), 227.

2. John 13.34; cf. John 15.12.

3. George Scholarios, "Peri Eleemosynes," ed. L. Petit, X.A. Siderides and Martin Jugie, *Oeuvres Complètes de Georges Scholarios,* 1 (Paris, 1928), 100.

4. Irenaios, *Adversus Haereses,* Bk. IV, 38.1; Athanasios, *Against the Arians,* 1. 39.

5. Luke 4:18.

6. John 3:16.

7. Gregory Nazianzenos, "Homily 14.14," *PG* 35:1, 876.

8. Nicholas Kabasilas, *Eis ten Theian Leitourgian,* 17. 4, ed. S. Salaville; 2nd. ed. by R. Bornert *et al.,* Sources Chrétiennes (Paris, 1967), p. 134.

9. George Scholarios, "Peri ton kat'Areten Ergon," *Oeuvres Completes,* 3, 419-420.

10. Galatians 5.6.

11. John Chrysostom, "Postremo de Lazaro mendico ac de Divite," *PG* 48:1029.

12. See my *Byzantine Philanthropy and Social Welfare,* Rutgers Byzantine Series (New Brunswick, N.J., 1968), pp. 18-28., 88-110.

13. Matthew 26.26-29; John 6.32-59; I Corinthians 11.20-34.

14. John of Damascus, *De Fide Orthodoxa, PG* 94:1. 1153A; cf. John Chrysostom, "Homily 46," *PG* 59: 260.

15. See my *Byzantine Philanthropy,* pp. 154-55, 74-75; also my article "Life and Social Welfare Activity of Patriarch Athanasios I...of Constantinople," *Theologia,* 46 (1975), 611-25. For Theoleptos, see my forthcoming article "Mysticism and Social Involvement in the Late Byzantine Church..." in *Byzantine Studies.*

16. Gregory Palamas, *Logoi Apodeiktikoi Dyo—Logos Deuteros,* 78, ed. P.K. Christou *et al.,* vol. 1, p. 149.

17. Photios, "Homily 2.3," ed. B. Laourdas, *Photiou Homiliai* (Thessalonike, 1959), p. 15.

18. Irenaios, *Fragments,* no. 10, in *Library of the Greek Fathers and Ecclesiastical Writers,* 5 (Athens, 1955), 175.

19. Photios, "Homily 2.4" *Photiou Homiliai,* p. 17.

20. Nicholas Kabasilas, *Peri tes en Christo Zoes,* ed. W. Gass, *Die Mystik des Nikolaus Cabasilas vom Leben in Christo,* pp. 153-56, 160-62, 165-67.

21. 1 Corinthians 5.5.

IS THERE A FUTURE FOR AN EASTERN RITE CATHOLICISM IN THE UNITED STATES?

by

PHILIP A. KHAIRALLAH

During the late middle ages, after the complete rejection of the Council of Florence by the Eastern Churches, it looked as though the Catholic Church was becoming entirely a Latin institution and that Roman Catholicism was becoming synonymous with the Western Church. At that time there were only two small eastern bodies still in communion with the Church of Rome, namely the Byzantine Greeks in Italy and Sicily and the Maronites in Lebanon. At different times after the rejection of the Council of Florence varying bodies, small and large, of Eastern Christians began to return to communion with the Church of Rome. In 1595 took place the union of Brest Litovsk when the Metropolitan of Kiev and some of his bishops of Southwest Russia and Poland reestablished communion, followed in the middle of the 17th century by a further group of Byzantine Slavs primarily from the southern part of the Ukraine and Czechoslovakia. In 1698 part of the Orthodox Church in Romania, one Bishop with his clergy and people "united and confessed themselves to be members of the Holy Catholic and Roman Church." Finally, in 1724 the Church of Antioch was divided, some entering into communion with Rome while others electing their own hierarchs, thus setting up two rival Melkite patriarchs and two lines of hierarchs.

Starting in the late 19th century numerous eastern rite Catholics began immigrating into the United States and Canada. Many of those of Slavic background settled in Pennsylvania and Ohio while those of middle eastern background settled in Boston and New York. Although complete statistics are not available, since many of the faithful who settle in areas where no churches of their rite existed have disappeared, it is estimated that at present there are between two and two and one half million Catholics of the Byzantine rite, also called Uniates. The larger bodies present have their own hierarchs and jurisdiction, the Ukranian Catholic Church with a metropolitan in Philadephia, Pennsylvania and two diocesan bishops in Stamford, Connecticut and Chicago, Illinois; Catholics of the Ruthenian rite also have three dioceses, a metropolitan residing in Pittsburgh, Pennsylvania, and diocesan bishops in Passaic, New Jersey, and Parma, Ohio. The Melkites have one diocese covering all of the United States with a bishop residing in West Newton, Massachusetts, while the Romanians and Russians have no residential hierarchs and are dependent upon the local Roman rite bishops.

Although at the time of rejoining communion with the Roman Catholic Church the eastern hierarchs and people received solemn promises that they would retain the fullness of their eastern tradition, varying degrees of Latinization have crept in; so much so that these eastern Catholic Churches have essentially become, by the first half of the 20th century, Roman Catholic Churches which have a few quaint customs remaining, and who celebrate Mass in a quaint and different way.

Numerous examples can be cited of both Latinization of the Eastern Catholic Churches and the way Rome, through the Sacred Congregation for the Oriental Churches, has treated these Eastern Catholic Churches. One recent example may be illustrative. On 30 September 1977, the Roman Synod on Catechesis was opened by a concelebrated liturgy presided over by Pope Paul VI. Patriarch Maximos V of Antioch represented the Melkite Church at this Synod. When he arrived in the Sistine Chapel for the opening liturgy he was asked to sit at the back of the chapel behind Roman rite bishops and priests. Patriarch Maximos V and the Syriac rite Patriarch Hayek and Joseph Slipj, major archbishop of the Ukranians, walked out. The reason for this walkout was to bring to the attention of the world the role of patriarchs and major archbishops of Eastern Churches united with Rome. This had been hammered out at Vatican II, where the Eastern Catholic patriarchs and major archbishops were seated at the right of the aula on the opposite side of the aisle from the cardinals of the Roman Catholic Church. Although this incident has been passed over to questions of protocol, it has a much deeper significance because it is typical of the role Eastern Catholic Churches feel is their due, and the actual situation with which Rome treats these quaint relics supposedly representing the fullness of Byzantium. This is to be contrasted to the reception of Patriarch Athenagoras of Constatninople in 1965, or to the astounding picture of Pope Paul VI kissing the foot of Bishop Meliton in 1976. Archibishop Elias Zoghby, Melkite Greek Catholic Archbishop of Baalbeck, has reported, "Over the years since our reunion with Rome (1724), Rome has allowed us to retain the titles of Patriarch and Bishops that are still being used in the Orthodox Church. We now recognize that these titles are just titles with no concomitant authority. The Patriarchal Synod, which is the basis of Orthodox ecclesiology, no longer has any real authority among us. All of its decisions can be modified or annulled by different Roman congregations, especially the Sacred Congregation for the Oriental Churches. This Roman congregation supervising all of the Eastern Catholic Patriarchates acts in a way similar to a Super Patriarch, since it has the last word in any and all affairs affecting the separate oriental Patriarchates. Up until now most of the Eastern Catholic clergy have been trained by western teachers imparting to them western theology and western canon law. The western Church has ignored the whole institutiton of the Patriarchate and the Synodal system of functioning in the Church. Thus, recent Popes of Rome have only found one way in which to honor the eastern Catholic Patriarchs and this is to name them Cardinals."[1]

What is the future of the Eastern Catholic Churches, especially those in the United States? Three main trends seem to be contributing to tensions within these churches. A great majority of the Eastern Catholics, including many clergy and some hierarchs, especially those trained in seminaries before the latter half of the 1960's, cannot shake themselves free from the intellectual domination of Rome. These people see no danger in a very close dependence upon Roman Catholic philosophy and theology and, to make matters worse, these individuals see nothing wrong with this. This problem is further compounded since many of the children of eastern Catholics study in Latin parochial schools, grade school, high school and even at a college level. In spite of the best intentions, these children become totally Latinized and slowly, by the time they reach adulthood, disappear. This group fully equates the concept of rite to that of external rubrics used in celebrating the Eucharistic Sacrifice. For them the Divine Liturgy and few other liturgical services still celebrated have been detached from the body of faith as expressed in the Eastern Church or community, the local church, and have grafted on to another local church (the Roman Church). This is what these individuals understand the word rite to mean. This group can only disappear, swallowed up by the preponderant majortiy of the western church. To this group problems in ecumenism, especially Roman Catholic-Orthodox relations, seem to be very insignificant since to them Rome is always right and everyone else, to varying degrees, is wrong. Reconciliation with the Orthodox Churches is simple since they state that both Churches share the same liturgy and beliefs with the exception of the role of the Pope in the united church and maybe a few other "minor" problems such as the immaculate conception, purgatory and the procession of the Holy Spirit. These individuals feel that they can easily convince the Orthodox that these minor questions can be settled by convincing them of the reasonableness of the Roman position.

A second trend can be distinguished. This seems to be the official point of view since many of the hierarchs follow this line. In the United States it more closely characterizes the position of the Melkite diocese and somewhat less so of the Ukranian and Ruthenian dioceses. This group maintains that it is possible to place oriental Catholicism in such a way as to maintain what is best of both Orthodox and Catholic traditions. They make a good case for the necessity of some expression of Eastern Catholicism and state that the role of Eastern Catholicism is to act as a bridge between Western Catholicism and eastern Orthodoxy. This group is trying to reintroduce some of the eastern traditions into the life of the church such as the regular celebration of vespers and matins, and is trying to combat the constant but slow process of Latinization still going on. This group has also made the word Orthodox known to the west. This group, however, has some major deficiences; since most of its leaders are still living the western theological training received in their seminaries, schools and, in the case of many of them, studies in Rome. Thus, although some of the basic theological issues are recognized, responses to the problems are still made in western thought patterns. Many of the clergy trained in seminaries in this country since the late 1960's are of this tradition and background, but this has also led to internal tensions. Just as an example, one seminary run by a religious order has had eight of its graduates ordained for an Eastern Catholic Church and eight others ordained for the Orthodox Church.

There is a third way of thinking, non-existent before Vatican II, and at present still a minority, but growing. This group feels that union with Rome either in 1595 or 1724 was a mistake, at least in hindsight. There have been valid reasons at those times, but the union with Rome that was entered into was primarily for short-term benefits. This group feels that the main function today of the Eastern Catholic Churches is to reconcile Rome with the east and to live the fullness of Orthodoxy still in communion with Roman Catholicism. This group sympathizes with the Orthodox statements that the Eastern Catholics were deserters, and today are a hindrance towards union instead of a link. The Orthodox feel that this group left them for what was considered to be greener pastures on the other side. The main aim of the group is to work for a closer involvement with the Orthodox Churches, leading to the eventual disappearance of their Eastern Catholic Churches, to reunite the Uniates with their mother church, the Orthodox. This group's ethos, spirituality and faith is much closer to the Orthodox Church than to the Roman Catholic Church of today. This group wants to do away with the Western concept of rite and instead thinks in terms of a local church with its own theology, exegesis, ecclesiology, spirituality, discipline, canon law and tradition. This local church in its fullness with its bishops and patriarch will try to remain in communion with the local Church of Rome

A Future for an Eastern Rite Catholicism in the U.S.?

and definitely not *under* the Church of Rome. This group finally feels that only two churches, the Latin Church in the west and the Orthodox Church in the east, possess the totality of Christian patrimony. These two patrimonies are complementary, not opposite, and the present role of the Eastern Catholic Churches is to make the western Church accept the fullness of the reality of the eastern Church. Until such a day as the western church can live in perfect harmony with their eastern Catholic brothers, only then can the western Church talk about reestablishing communion with the Orthodox Churches. The decree on the Catholic Churches of the eastern rite by Vatican II, in spite of its deficiencies, is a first step in the right direction. The time is here and now that the Sacred Congregation for the Oriental Churches reread this decreee and start implementing it. If this cannot occur in the near future, the only recourse left for this third group is to humbly ask forgiveness, and to be reintegrated with their mother Church, the Orthodox, not negating their past, but praying that the Holy Spirit may guide the western Church and let it see the vision of one reunited Body of Christ.

What of the future? Do the eastern Catholic Churches have a role to play within Roman Catholicism? It is the present writer's position that only the third position above is a viable alternative for the United States. The Roman Catholic Church will not gain anything by adding two million parishioners to its rolls. Many Roman Catholic faithful, in turn, very disenchanted with the liturgical life and spirituality of their community, are searching for something more "meaningful" and have been turning towards eastern Catholicism. It is only by living the fullness of the eastern Orthodox tradition that the eastern Catholics can justify their continued existence and at the same time welcome those disenchanted with their own church. Today Rome and Orthodoxy recognize themselves as sister churches not yet in perfect communion with one another. Since the eastern Catholic Churches are in full communion, they should insist on living as sister churches, retaining the fullness of their patrimony, living the fullness of the eastern Orthodox faith, while still in communion with the Church of Rome. They should actively work towards the eventual disappearance of their own eastern rites and their reintegration into the great churches of the east, of Constantinople, Alexandria, Antioch, Jerusalem and Moscow. Only thus can they justify their continued existence as a minority in a western country.

NOTES

1. *Proche Orient Chrétien,* 27(1977), pp. 371-74.

CARING FOR EQUIVALENTS

Comments on the Current Relations of Orthodox and Roman Catholics
by
ROBERT G. STEPHANOPOULOS

Father Georges Florovsky, the pre-eminent Orthodox historian and ecumenist, has described aptly the estrangement of Eastern and Western Christianity as a sore defeat of the 'catholicity' of mind once prevailing in the ancient undivided Church. There was a gradual disintegration of the common Christian tradition among the protagonists. "There was, indeed, little 'care for equivalents,' and little care for accurate rendering of the thoughts of others."[1]
As devastating as this mutual attitude of polemic partisanship and local loyalty was to the proper relationship between the two halves of Christendom, it must never be forgotten that the break was never absolute and irreversible. The common foundation has never been lost. It is on this basis that the hopeful rapprochement between the two is once again proceeding. The scandalous atmosphere of massive opposition and subtle distortion is slowly giving way to the irenic ethos of the modern ecumenical movement with its positive dynamism and joyful surprises of (re)discovery. There is a care for equivalents once again. Essential tools in this effort are the painstaking investigations of the historical, biblical and theological disciplines.
Throughout his patriarchal reign, the venerable Ecumenical Patriarch Athenagoras of Constantinople concentrated much of his attention on the issue of improving relations with the Roman Catholic Church.[2] Clearly, however, the impetus for the new climate was provided during the pontificate of the saintly and pastoral Pope John XXIII and of his eminent successor Pope Paul VI. Rome entered decisively and seriously into the ecumenical movement, and particularly into genuine dialogue

with the Orthodox Communion. For their part, each particular Orthodox Church, consistent with the principle of autocephaly and in agreement with the policy adopted at the Pan-Orthodox Conferences during the decade of the sixties, has espoused dialogue with Rome *in principle,* although each has retained the right to proceed at its own pace.[3]

The progress noted thus far is most encouraging. Good relations are proceeding in an atmosphere of charity, honesty and mutual good faith toward the purpose of complete understanding and eventual doctrinal and sacramental reconciliation. From the Roman Catholic perspective there is measured enthusiasm, reflected in both the official and unofficial theological literature, for the projected dialogue. Father Michael Fahey concludes a recent study by stating that Roman Catholic opinion reflects "a broad theoretical basis for recognizing more fully the ecclesial and sacramental life of both Churches."[4]

A similar measure of enthusiasm is seen within certain Orthodox circles. Metropolitan Chrysostom (Zapheiris), in a lengthy article on the developing dialogue between Constantinople and Rome, treats favorably the mutual proposal to deal with the sacramental themes as the point of departure for theological conversations. The 'dialogue of charity' is now moving beyond formal and symbolic good relations to a sweeping theoretical discussion of issues which both unite and separate the two communions.[5] All indications point toward the successful completion of a process which is both official and fully representative of the sister Churches in dialogue with one another.

This is especially remarkable in light of the great reservations of many Orthodox theologians expressed during and after the Second Vatican Council about the possibility of a dialogue with Rome "on equal terms"($\dot{\epsilon}\pi\grave{\iota}$ ἰσοῖς ὁροῖς).[6] Their real doubts that Rome could ever deal officially and in terms of equality with the Orthodox Churches prevented any unanimity of action at first. Only gradually did it become apparent that Vatican II had profoundly changed the internal life of the Roman Church, not so much in terms of what was promulgated in the documents, but rather in the effect they had in transforming the entire atmosphere of Roman Christianity.

Vatican II did a great deal to redirect the course of renewal in the Catholic Church in contemporary times. Much material has been provided for the confrontation of the challenges of the modern world and for some theological realignments. The ensuing upheaval in certain quarters of the Catholic Church has not seriously divided its faithful. The overwhelming majority of 'reformers' and interpreters of the Council's documents are dedicated and loyal Catholics who have no inclination to divide the Church or separate from it. The flexibility and pastoral resiliency displayed by the magisterium and the fidelity of the alerted faithful in every section of the Church has kept the spirit of the Church alive.[7] This is certainly a valuable and hopeful indication for the current stage of dialogue, since renewal efforts should not be the occasion for further fragmentation within the respective communions. Tensions within the Orthodox communion are certainly as widespread and dangerous, but there has been no serious breach as yet.[8]

There were numerous Orthodox critiques and reservations about the documents promulgated by Vatican II, particularly those dealing with the Eastern Churches, Ecumenism and the Church. In effect, they cover the agenda of issues in the current stage of theological dialogue between the two Churches.[9] But, there can be no question that without Vatican II the possibility for meaningful relations between the two Churches would be negligible.

Perhaps the best summary assessment of the high significance of Vatican II from the Orthodox perspective is provided by the noted Greek theologian and eucmenical scholar, Professor Nikos Nissiotis.[10] He cites the very fact of the Council as the best possible evidence of a desire within the heart of the Roman Church to return to the sources of the Christian tradition and the principle of conciliarity. The Council was an affirmation and a symbol of the fact that the conciliary institution is an intergral part of Catholic ecclesiology. All Church doctrine and practice must be interpreted in terms of this momentous event. This admission has provided the basis for reconciliation and reunion with separated Communions, as well as the possibility for the scrutiny of medieval developments in ecclesiology in the light of the ancient tradition.

The emphasis upon the collegiality of the Pope and the bishops, although not precisely located in the idea of the people of God and expressed in tandem with texts which confirm the primacy of the Pope, nevertheless provides for fresh interpretations of the meaning of the Christian community and the role of the primacy within that community.

An example of how this may be seen as a real step forward is provided in the 25 July 1967 brief of Pope Paul to Patriarch Athenagoras entitled *Anno ineunte*. Father John Meyendorff points out the significance of the use of the traditional Orthodox concept of "sister Churches" to describe the relations between the two at the present time, since the basis for mutual recognition is in the mystery of the sacramental presence of Christ in 'each local church.' He continues,

> this text seems to imply that the rapprochement between East and West must be understood as a *progressive mutual recognition of local churches,* (italics his) and not as a return to Roman 'obedience.'[11]

Of course, there is a real problem here, perhaps even a contradiction, which is implicit in such statements. The Petrine office is still regarded as final and absolute. There are numerous reminders in all of these statements that the very unity and authority of the Church is guaranteed and connected integrally to the Petrine office and ministry.

Nevertheless, the Roman authorities are apparently able to put forward their position fully cognizant of its inconsistencies. The ambiguity is there and the question must be asked in all charity whether it is a contradiction, and is it deliberate? Certainly, the answer must in its own good time be provided by Rome itself. The responsibility of all others is to continue to persevere in the hope that an ongoing dialogue informed by the content of the Christian Gospel and the Apostolic witness will reveal the true meaning of this perspective.

The truly positive signs must be seen in the Council teachings

Caring for Equivalents

on the mysterious nature of the Church, the biblical imagery of the Church as a sign placed by God in the midst of His people and the great importance given to the local churches and traditions.[12] Certainly the Eastern Churches have been acknowledged once again in the most solemn manner as *Churches*. There is now a basis for communion, however imperfectly it may be perceived for the time being. Moreover, there is the admission that grievous errors have been perpetrated on either side in the past. This may be problematical; it may present a crisis in authority in full view of the outside world; it may be introducing acutely the problem of theological pluralism. Nevertheless, Rome seems to be intent upon living with this ambiguity and pursuing its course of dialogue and reconciliation with the East.

The official Pan-Orthodox commitment to dialogue with Rome was proposed on 14 December 1975, by Metropolitan Meliton as the personal representative of Ecumenical Patriarch Demetrios I. The dramatic gesture of the ailing Pope Paul VI falling at the feet of the emissary of this good news said more than volumes could have done. It was a gesture, but one fraught with deep symbolic meaning. It showed graphically to a hesitant East that Rome profoundly desired dialogue with its sister Churches, nurtured in a climate of mutual respect and equality and aimed at eventual full communion.

The importance of official texts and pronouncements is paramount. But, their interpretation and reception is very often dependent upon the actions and gestures of the notables of the two Churches. Style and attitude are as important as what is said in the letter; these communicate even more effectively than language itself. Therefore,

> the public *image* of a pope appearing in Istanbul and in Rome as a *brother* (and therefore ontologically an *equal* of another bishop) cannot be reduced to mere diplomacy or protocol. The well-known definitions of papal supremacy were in no way denounced, of course, but neither were they publicly expressed in any way. Facing the Orthodox, the pope presented himself with the function of *primus inter pares* ('first among equals') which the Orthodox had recognized in him in the past.[13]

There has been no lack of such deeply symbolic actions and gestures. By now the official exchange of letters, delegations and theological position papers is almost routine. The solemn service of nullification and lifting of the anathemas of 1054, although certainly not of a canonical nature, gave expression to the hope that there is a sincere desire for reconciliation on the part of both Churches.

The official dialogue, now more than ever, puts a special responsibility on the Orthodox. Rome has made deliberate and specific steps to insure its success. The Orthodox in turn must reciprocate in a manner which is befitting the solemnity of the dialogue process and which is consistent with its own self-awareness.

Perhaps the first area of concentration for Orthodox is that of reviewing our papacy 'paranoia.' Just as papal primacy and infallibility in the West have undergone a development, sometimes incorrectly articulated and misapplied, so there has in the East been a corresponding massive opposition to any development. The voices of understanding and balanced appreciation were few and all too feeble. Recognition must be given to the genuine efforts of Roman theologians to review the developments in the West's perception of the papacy. Sound theological reflection on our part can dispel the notion that Roman Catholic ecclesiology is monolithic on this question and that the centrality of Rome is reducible to a simple lust for power. Catholic theology is much more consciously pluralistic and diversified than Orthodox are wont to suspect. There are remarkable efforts at self-articulation and clarification constantly going on. Current ecumenical ideas proposed about the Petrine office and ministry are certainly less triumphalistic and much more conciliary than they were in even the very recent past. Catholics are much more sensitive than ever to the voices of caution and correction, both within their ranks and without.

The nature of the Church, its unity and catholicity and mission, are at the heart of our present state of division as Church communities. The single outstanding example of such an ecclesiological problem is that of the status and function of the Pope in expressing and furthering the unity of the universal church in its mission to the world. Orthodox must be reminded that the Petrine ministry like all the other ministries of the church is a gift of God, given for the good order of the institutional church which must be visibly united. Our common tradition supports the thesis that this Petrine ministry was a ministry of good order, a service of solicitude and loving care of the elder brother for the other members of the family of God. Seen as a ministry of love and unity, the papacy is considerably less threatening and objectionable.[14]

Furthermore, the Orthodox must reduce their own tendency to triumphalize and give the appearance of a monolith. Our statements are too often given to high sounding idealism only barely corresponding to real conditions. There are ambiguities and inconsistencies in Orthodox theology as well, particularly as these relate to ecclesiology.[15]

Certainly the psychological climate among the Orthodox is not as open to dialogue with Rome as one would wish. Efforts at understanding through local and regional ecumenical programs are minimal. Ecumenism is too often regarded as a new form of subversion and the eventual submission of Orthodoxy to Rome. The lingering problem of "Uniatism" is far from resolved, but no matter how it may be interpreted by others, almost all Orthodox see it as an instrument of ecclesiastical imperialism and a medium of proselytization. Unless this problem is seen in its true ecclesiological dimensions, it will continue to be an open sore further poisoning the relations between the two Churches.

In the final analysis, the dialogue of charity between Roman Catholicism and Orthodoxy rests on the mutual expressions in practice of the reality to which both communions claim to bear witness. This is an eminently 'ecumenical' task, in the sense that it speaks to the universe in space and time which is the Christian Tradition. The ecumenical experience of both communions has brought them to a point of mutual respect in their relations. Certain policies and schemes are no longer applicable to the advancement of real unity. What is clear is that good will is not sufficient to the task, although it is fundamental. A more representative and profound listening to the common tradition is required. It is in the unity of the Apostolic witness, through constant reference to the sources of divine Revelation itself, that Christian unity is to be recovered. The one faith is the basis for recognizing the true Church and the sacraments, not compromise or doctrinal minimalism and 'artificial intercommunion.' True humanity and true community are rooted in the one Church which has its origins and its destiny in the Trinity rather than in the transient ideologies of the present age. It is fidelity to this theocentric perspective that will lead us out of our present state of division into the fulness of ecclesial communion.

NOTES

1. "The Problem of Ecumenical Encounter," in E. L. B. Fry and A. H. Armstrong, editors, *Rediscovering Eastern Christendom: Essays in Memory of Dom Bede,* Winslow (London, 1963), pp. 65-66.

2. See my unpublished dissertation, Robert G. Stephanopoulos, *A Study in Recent Greek Orthodox Ecumenical Relations, 1902-1968* (Ph. D. dissertation, Boston University, 1970), pp. 289 ff., and *Tomos Agapis: Vatican-Phanar (1958-1970)* (Rome, 1971), passim.

3. Stephanopoulos, *Study,* pp. 275 ff., for the problems issuing out of the Second Vatican Council and the Pan-Orthodox Conferences.

4. Michael A. Fahey, S. J., "Reconciliation between Orthodoxy and Catholicism: A Roman Catholic View," *Diakonia* 10(1975), 10.

5. As reported in *Episkepsis* (Biweekly Bulletin published by the Orthodox Centre of the Ecumenical Patriarchate: Chambesy, Geneva) No. 192 (1/1/78), 13-16 (in Greek).

6. Stephanopoulos, *A Study,* pp. 293 ff. and 302 ff.

7. Certain negative signs notwithstanding, for example. the despairing mood of Dutch Roman Catholicism as its efforts at renewal are frustrated. Cf. Michael Miles, "The Winter Mood of Dutch Catholicism," *The Christian Century,* vol. 95, no. 35 (1 Nov. 1978), 1038-1044.

8. The traditionalist and conservative anti-ecumenical groups within Orthodoxy are numerous and highly vocal. See, for example, the publications of the Russian Orthodox Church in Exile and the Greek polemical literature in Stephanopoulos, *Study,* pp. 299 ff. and 305.

9. Cf. Michael A. Fahey, S. J., "Orthodox Ecumenism and Theology: 1970-78," *Theological Studies,* 39 (1978), 446-85, for a review of Orthodox theological issues, particularly as they touch upon Roman Catholicism.

10. "What Still Separates Us from the Catholic Church? An Orthodox Reply," in *Post-Ecumenical Christianity,* Hans Kung, *Concilium,* vol. 54 (New York, 1970), 28-29.

11. John Meyendorff, *A Pope for All Christians? An Inquiry into the Role of Peter in the Modern Church,* ed. Peter J. McCord (New York, 1976), pp. 139 ff.

12. Stylianos Hartkianakis, "The Ecclesiology of Vatican II: An Orthodox Summary," *Diakonia* 2/3 (1967), 238.

13. John Meyendorff, *Orthodoxy and Catholicity* (New York, 1966), p. 138.

14. Robert G. Stephanopoulos, "Christian Unity and the Petrine Ministry: Remarks of an Orthodox Christian," *Journal of Ecumenical Studies,* 11 (1974), 309-14.

15. Fahey, "Reconciliation," pp. 15-19.